MOVEABLE FEAST

with **fine Cooking**

INSPIRING RECIPES
FROM SEASONS 1 AND 2

The Taunton Press

WGBH

© 2015 WGBH Educational Foundation and
The Taunton Press, Inc.

The Taunton Press
Inspiration for hands-on living®

WGBH

The Taunton Press, Inc., 63 South Main Street, PO Box 5506,
Newtown, CT 06470-5506 e-mail: tp@taunton.com

Editor: Nanette Maxim
Copy editor: Nina Rynd Whitnah
Jacket/cover design: Sandy Mahlstedt
Interior design and layout: Rita Sowins
Photography art director: Teresa Fernandes
Food stylist: Ronne Day
Photographers: Colin Clark: 6, 16, 17, 18, 19, 20, 21, 22, 23, 24,
25, 28, 34, 35, 39, 44 (top right), 52, 53, 54, 55, 56, 58, 59, 60, 61,
204, 214, 215, 217, 218, 221, 222, 223, 225, 226, 228, 229, 230,
232, 233; Scott Phillips: 9 (bottom left), 10, 13, 14, 26, 29, 30, 33,
36, 41, 42, 47, 49, 50, 62 (bottom right), 64, 67, 68, 70, 73, 83,
84, 89, 93, 94, 97, 98, 101, 105 (top left), 106, 109, 113, 118, 119,
121, 122, 125, 130, 132, 135, 137, 138, 145 (bottom left), 147,
148, 151, 154, 157, 160, 167, 168, 173, 177, 180, 182, 185, 186,
188, 189, 190 (bottom left), 192, 195, 196, 200, 203, 209, 210,
213, 220; Melina Hammer: 107; courtesy Redwood Hill Farm: 163

All recipes appearing in *Moveable Feast with Fine Cooking* have
been adapted by the *Fine Cooking* Test Kitchen.

Library of Congress Cataloging-in-Publication Data

Moveable feast with Fine cooking : inspiring recipes from seasons 1
and 2 / editors of Fine cooking.
       pages cm
   Includes index.
   ISBN 978-1-63186-373-8
1. Cooking, American. I. Moveable feast with Fine cooking
(Television program) II. Taunton's fine cooking.
   TX715.M 91849 2015
   641.5973--dc23
                                    2015025848

Printed in the United States of America
10 9 8 7 6 5 4 3 2 1

CONTENTS

PREFACE

Does the world really need another television show about food and cooking? When we set out to create a *Fine Cooking* TV show, we thought long and hard about how to make it stand out from all the other programs for and about people who love food.

We knew that the way we do things at *Fine Cooking* is different. We inspire cooks and deepen their knowledge with expert how-to advice and amazing recipes. Whether it's a chef's variation on grilled cheese or learning the secrets to succulent barbecue shrimp, we lead readers on a culinary exploration. We knew we could take our unique sense of discovery and passion for cooking and do on television what we've been doing in print and online for so many years.

And so with the help of our partner, WGBH in Boston, *Moveable Feast with Fine Cooking* was born. For three seasons we've taken viewers on culinary journeys across the U.S., from Portland, Maine, to Portland, Oregon, joined by some of the area's best chefs, purveyors, food artisans, and farmers. Drawing on all that makes each region sing, the chefs create a pop-up feast while racing against the clock to prepare and share with friends and family. And they introduce us to the folks that make food in the region special and share favorite cooking tips and techniques along the way. We're happy to say that this approach has struck a chord. *Moveable Feast with Fine Cooking* has garnered many awards and accolades, including an Emmy award nomination for Outstanding Culinary Series, three Telly Awards, a Taste Award for our programming, as well as a James Beard nomination for Best Host.

Putting together a show like this takes the talents of many, foremost our co-producers at WGBH, Director of Lifestyle Programming Laurie Donnelly and Senior Program Producer Anne Adams, whose guidance and expertise helped to shape the concept and then turn it into a lively reality. There's host Pete Evans, with his sense of adventure and mean cooking chops; our many guest chefs; an outstanding crew, including Director Rob Tate, Producers Mimi Adams and Lauren Thompson, Culinary Producer Nora Singley, our *Fine Cooking* team, and many others. And a special thanks to our Season 1 and 2 funders, Colavita®, Saber Grill®, and Sun Maid®, for their generous support.

We at *Fine Cooking* are so proud of *Moveable Feast*. Thanks to all of you at home who have made our show a success.

Fine Cooking **Editors**

INTRODUCTION

What makes a "moveable feast"? For writer Ernest Hemingway, who coined the phrase in his memoir of Paris in the 1920s, it was a vibrant city where around every corner there was something magical to be discovered, where there were people to eat and drink with, to sit around a table and talk and laugh and argue with, to dive deeply into life.

It's an idea we wanted to translate to a show that takes you around the country, to sample the best that America's growers and cooks have to offer and the joy they take in making the most of their corner of the world. The notion of a moveable feast seems a perfect fit.

Sharing the "foraging" for a meal, as well as cooking and eating it, is one of life's great pleasures—whether that means fishing on the Mississippi Delta, as we did with New Orleans chefs Donald Link and Stephen Stryjewski, or cooking polenta that's been ground just down the road at a 200-year-old gristmill, as we did in the Napa Valley with father-and-son chefs Larry and Marc Forgione. Or gathering eggs from very happy free-range chickens in Connecticut with the inimitable chef Jacques Pépin, who then delicately scrambled them with herbs he picked from the same farm.

The thing is, this isn't a one-off experience for these chefs. It's a way of life. They have relationships with the growers, the butchers, the cheese-makers, and the spice merchants. They're neighbors, and there's a feeling of community that comes from a mutual respect for ingredients and the hard work it takes to produce them.

It's been a voyage of discovery for me, right along with all of you who traveled with us from episode to episode. I was taught the art of handling a clam fork with grillmasters Chris Schlesinger and "Doc" Willoughby in Westport, Massachusetts, where I not only learned how to "quahog" but also how to pronounce it. We hit the Puget Sound for Dungeness crab with Seattle's dynamic duo Tom Douglas and Thierry Rautureau, foraged for wild greens in Portland, Maine, with Rob Evans and Sam Hayward, and strolled among grapevines at California wineries, as well as, surprisingly,

4

at a Massachusetts winery. In a hidden Pacific cove, we set a table that stretched as far as the eye could see, and as the waves lapped at our feet, chef Ravi Kapur fed us salmon freshly caught by fisherman Hans Haveman.

We met some of the next generation of chefs at one of the great U.S. cooking schools, The Culinary Institute of America at Greystone, with the "Godfather of American Cuisine," Larry Forgione. And we cooked rich *sugo* with the "Queen of Pork," Chef Duskie Estes of Zazu, in Healdsburg, California. Then we hunted for great Asian ingredients at Chicago's family-run Joong Boo Market with "the Girl," Chef Stephanie Izard, of Girl & the Goat restaurant.

One minute we were in New York's Little Italy eating capocollo at Di Palo's, which carries on the legacy of the small butchers and dairies that made the neighborhood great. The next, we were cooking with the likes of Leo Beckerman and Evan Bloom, whose Wise Sons Deli feels as if they took the Lower East Side of New York and transplanted it to the West Coast.

And whether we were in Harlem, New York, or Buchanan, Michigan, there was food that was cooked with love and a sense of place. So we've collected these fantastic recipes from seasons one and two to share with you, to re-create the good times we had on the road, and to bring them into your own kitchen. They're a taste of America, and of the best that America is cooking now, region by region. We hope they inspire you to keep the feast going by throwing one of your own.

Pete Evans

NORTHEAST

For cooks in the Northeast, the region offers a crazy quilt of riches. With the Atlantic on one side and rich farmland on the other, and New England pastoral meeting New York City urban, it's about as diverse as the country gets.

Northeast chefs, too, are as diverse as the cities they hale from. But what they all have in common is a deep respect for what the land provides. We cooked with the best of the best on our *Moveable Feast* Northeast trips, and the recipes on these pages offer a delicious sampler.

Life on the water looms large in the region, and we progressed on a search for the finest Atlantic seafood out there with some of the area's most skilled fishermen and the seafood cooks who depend on them. In Portland, Maine, chefs Rob Evans and Sam Hayward take us on an excursion to mussel growers from Bangs Island. A day in Westport, Massachusetts, spent clamming (or "quahogging" as it's called in the area) with grillmasters John "Doc" Willoughby and Chris Schlesinger results in fresher than fresh shellfish cooked over an open fire. And in Duxbury, Massachusetts, a bounty of oysters, mackerel, and lobster become the ultimate beach picnic. Fishing for black bass and whelk off Long Island's North Fork, leads chefs Bill Taibe and Will Horowitz to throw an old-fashioned New England clambake.

Inland we explore (and forage) field and farm to discover wild greens, sustainably raised pigs, sheep, and cattle, and even a vineyard where people said it was madness to plant grapes (they were wrong). Legendary chef Jacques Pépin gathers fresh eggs (and scrambles them with herbs and tomatoes) at Wilton, Connecticut's Millstone Farm, and Tim LaBant scoops honey straight from the hive; meanwhile, Bill Taibe tends to roast pork in the kitchen.

And then there's the siren call of New York, New York, where the cooking is a little like jazz. Chef Marcus Samuelsson employs the sounds (and farmers' market) of Harlem to serve up an urban feast at Ginny's Supper Club, along with downtown chef Jonathan Waxman, whose gnocchi can melt in your mouth.

Downtown, in Little Italy, artisan cheeses and meats are an integral part of the Italian-American culinary landscape. It's where older producers (Di Palo's) and new (Il Laboratorio del Gelato) co-exist and chefs like Marco Canora and Gabrielle Hamilton bring them all together at the table.

"There's something about the spell of being on a Maine island that makes just about anything that comes out of it terrific."

—Sam Hayward

PORTLAND, MAINE

Maine's bounty, from land and sea, takes center stage in this Down East feast. Award-winning chefs Rob Evans and Sam Hayward, two of Portland's champions of area farmers and fishermen, gather mussels from Bangs Island, then take a field trip (literally) with master forager Evan Strusinski, at Flanagan's Farm, to pick daisies, clover, wild strawberries, and sheep sorrel that will give their food a wild touch. Eating from your own backyard, in the case of Portland, is easy to do.

FEAST FAVORITES

Beer-Steamed Mussels
SAM HAYWARD, Fore Street Grill

Casarecce Ragù with Ricotta
ROB EVANS, Duckfat restaurant

Rainbow Chard and Russian Kale with King Oyster Mushrooms and Bacon
SAM HAYWARD

Beer-Steamed Mussels

★ SAM HAYWARD   SERVES 6 AS A MAIN DISH OR 10 AS A FIRST COURSE

12 oz. bottle of wheat beer

6 lb. mussels, scrubbed clean
and debearded

3 Tbs. apple-cider vinegar

Sea salt and freshly ground
black pepper

1½ oz. (3 Tbs.) cold unsalted
butter, cut into ½-inch cubes

½ cup coarsely chopped mixed
herbs, such as rosemary,
chives, savory, thyme,
sorrel, and/or parsley, plus
additional for garnish

1 French baguette, cut into
½-inch-thick slices and
toasted

CHOOSING MUSSELS

Fresh mussels should
look tightly closed or
just slightly gaping open.
Make sure their shells are
closed or that they close
immediately with a gentle
tap. That's an indication
that they're still alive.
Once you have them in
hand, take a sniff. They
should smell like the
sea. If they're really fishy
smelling, don't buy them.

When creating this butter sauce, Chef Hayward stressed the importance of restraint when cooking with mussels: "Keep it simple to let them sing." He used sheep's sorrel as part of the herb blend, which has a lemon-like acidity.

In a 10-quart stockpot with a tight-fitting lid, bring the beer to a boil. Add the mussels, cover, and cook, tossing occasionally, until the mussels have completely opened, about 8 to 12 minutes. Discard any unopened shells. Transfer the mussels to a very large wide bowl and cover with foil.

Strain the cooking liquid through a fine-mesh strainer lined with a damp paper towel into a 3-quart saucepan. Add the vinegar and salt and pepper to taste and bring to a boil. Let the sauce cook to meld the flavors and reduce slightly, about 3 minutes.

Remove from the heat and whisk in the butter, a few cubes at a time, until all the butter has been added and the sauce is emulsified. Stir in the herbs and season to taste with salt and pepper.

Spoon the sauce over the mussels and garnish with more herbs. Serve with the bread to sop up the sauce.

— Bangs Island Mussels —

It's the cool water temperature and high nutrient availability in Maine's Casco Bay that make Bangs Island Mussels so plump, sweet, and tender, say owners Matt Moretti and his dad, Gary. Together, father and son put an emphasis on sustainable practices and increasing production, from collecting the mussel seed and setting the ropes to using energy-efficient vessels for harvesting (which they do all year round). In April 2014, Bangs Island had its first harvest of sugar kelp, which it now grows along with the mussels.

Matt keeps his eyes on the future, not only of his mussels business but also of a new generation of aquaculturists. As he told a reporter from Working Waterfront, "We want to focus on what grows naturally, and determine what we can do to foster that growth in an aquaculture setting. I want to see kids not lose that option."

Casarecce Ragù with Ricotta

★ ROB EVANS   SERVES 4 TO 6

2 cups fresh coarse
  breadcrumbs

3 Tbs. extra-virgin olive oil

Kosher salt and freshly ground
  black pepper

1½ lb. ground beef, not lean

1 large Vidalia onion, finely
  diced (about 2 cups)

4 medium cloves garlic, minced

1½ tsp. ground coriander

½ tsp. sweet paprika

½ tsp. ground cumin

½ tsp. Espelette pepper

1½ cups dry white wine

28-oz. can diced tomatoes,
  preferably San Marzano

2½ cups lower-salt chicken
  broth

1 oz. (2 Tbs.) unsalted butter

1 lb. dried casarecce,
  maccheroni, penne rigate, or
  fusilli pasta

½ cup ricotta

½ cup baby arugula leaves

1 Tbs. chopped fresh oregano

Grated Parmigiano-Reggiano,
  for serving

Casarecce is a short rolled pasta whose scroll-like shape invites sauces into its every nook and cranny. Chef Evans made his original ragù with ground goat meat and a home-made goat's-milk ricotta, which, if they're available in your area, are worth trying for their earthy flavor.

Position a rack in the center of the oven and heat the oven to 325°F.

Put the crumbs on a large rimmed baking sheet, toss with 1 Tbs. of the oil, and sprinkle with salt and pepper to taste. Toast until light golden and crisp, about 5 minutes. Let cool completely.

In a 6-quart Dutch oven or heavy-duty pot, heat 1 Tbs. of the oil on medium-high heat until shimmering. Add the ground beef, breaking it up with the back of a wooden spoon. Cook the beef, stirring occasionally and continuing to break up the meat, until it is dark brown and there is very little liquid left in the pan, about 12 minutes. Transfer to a plate with a slotted spoon.

Reduce the heat to medium, add the remaining 1 Tbs. oil to the pot, and heat until shimmering. Add the onion and cook until golden brown, about 10 minutes. Stir in the garlic, coriander, paprika, cumin, and Espelette pepper and cook until fragrant, about 1 minute.

Pour in the wine and, using a wooden spoon, scrape up the brown bits on the bottom of the pot; cook until the liquid is reduced by half, about 5 minutes.

Add the ground beef back to the pot, along with any juices. Add the tomatoes and ½ cup of the broth and bring to a boil, stirring frequently and crushing the tomatoes with the back of the spoon. Reduce the heat to a simmer and partially cover the pot with the lid. Simmer for 2 to 4 hours, stirring occasionally and adding the remaining chicken broth ½ cup at a time to replenish the evaporated liquid if the meat becomes dry. The ragù should be thick but pourable. Simmer uncovered for the last 30 minutes, stirring frequently, and season to taste with salt and pepper. Remove from the heat and stir in the butter until it is completely melted.

Meanwhile, bring a large pot of well-salted water to a boil. Add the pasta and cook according to the package directions until al dente.

To serve, transfer the cooked pasta to a large serving bowl. Add 1 cup of the ragù to the pasta and toss. Top with the remaining ragù and dollop with heaping tablespoons of the ricotta. Garnish with the arugula, breadcrumbs, and oregano. Serve with the Parmigiano on the side.

Rainbow Chard and Russian Kale with King Oyster Mushrooms and Bacon

★ SAM HAYWARD

SERVES 6 TO 8 AS A SIDE DISH

6 oz. slab bacon, cut into ½-inch-thick by 2-inch-long pieces

½ cup beer

1 Tbs. malt vinegar

14 oz. rainbow chard, washed, stemmed, and cut into bite-size pieces

14 oz. Russian kale, washed, stemmed, and cut into bite-size pieces

½ oz. (1 Tbs.) unsalted butter

6 oz. scallions, white parts only, roots trimmed

5 oz. king oyster mushrooms, sliced ¼-inch thick lengthwise

Kosher salt and freshly ground black pepper

⅓ cup lower-salt chicken broth

The large king oyster mushroom that Chef Hayward cooks with is one of the meatiest out there, but don't confuse it with its cousin, the regular oyster mushroom, which is shaped like a shell. If you can't find king oyster mushrooms, you can substitute shiitake mushrooms or sliced portabella caps.

Bring a 2-quart saucepan of water to a boil. Add the slab bacon and cook until slightly pale, about 3 minutes, this reduces the saltiness of the meat. Transfer to a paper-towel-lined plate to drain.

Place a steamer basket into a 6-quart stockpot with a tight-fitting lid. Add the beer and vinegar and bring to a boil over medium-high heat. Add the chard and kale, cover, and steam until the greens become tender, about 5 minutes. Remove from the heat and uncover.

Meanwhile, in a 12-inch skillet over medium-high heat, add the bacon pieces and cook until golden brown, about 2 minutes per side. Transfer to a paper-towel-lined plate and set aside.

Melt the butter in the skillet and add the scallions. Cook, stirring often, until they begin to soften, about 2 minutes. Add the mushrooms, and salt and pepper to taste. Cook, stirring occasionally, until the scallions and the mushrooms are golden, about 4 minutes. Add the chicken broth and scrape up any brown bits on the bottom of the pan. Add the chard and kale to the skillet and cook until heated through. Season to taste with salt and pepper.

To serve, transfer the greens and mushroom mixture to a large serving plate and top with the bacon.

"Here we call all hard-shell clams 'quahogs' [pronounced ko-hog]. And instead of 'clamming,' we say 'quahogging.' Every quahogger has his spot." —**Chris Schlesinger**

WESTPORT, MA

When the writing duo of Boston chef Chris Schlesinger and former *Gourmet* magazine executive editor John "Doc" Willoughby published their eighth book, *Grill It!*, in 2010, the *New York Times* dubbed them "the high priests of chicken thighs, cowboy steaks, and the spice drawers of the Caribbean and North Africa." The two men made the grill their grail with the James Beard–award-winning book *The Thrill of the Grill* in 1990, and haven't stopped playing with fire ever since. Wading in the shallows of the Westport River and digging for clams is how many a meal begins for grill masters Schlesinger and Willoughy. They also tap into the flavors of the local Portuguese community—whose fishermen are a vital part of New England history—for a seafood and sausage dish that honors the men, the culture, and the sea.

FEAST FAVORITES

Grilled Littlenecks Johnson

CHRIS SCHLESINGER AND JOHN "DOC" WILLOUGHBY, ADAPTED FROM CHEF STEVE JOHNSON

Grilled Sweet Potatoes with Molasses Glaze

JOHN "DOC" WILLOUGHBY

Grilled Bluefish with Smoky Chouriço Relish

CHRIS SCHLESINGER

Grilled Littlenecks Johnson

★ CHRIS SCHLESINGER AND JOHN "DOC" WILLOUGHBY   SERVES 4 TO 6 AS A FIRST COURSE

3 dozen littleneck clams, scrubbed well

6 oz. (12 Tbs.) unsalted butter

⅓ cup dry white wine

1 Tbs. minced garlic (2 large cloves)

2 tsp. smoked paprika

1 lemon, halved

3 Tbs. chopped fresh flat-leaf parsley

A simple combination of ingredients lets the littleneck clams (or quahogs, as they're called in Westport, Massachusetts) shine. Schlesinger and Willoughby attribute the recipe to their friend chef Steve Johnson (of Tiverton, Rhode Island, restaurant The Red Dory).

Heat a gas grill or prepare a charcoal grill with one half on medium high, and the other half on medium low. If your gas grill's heat is controlled front to back, heat on high for 5 minutes, then reduce to medium.

Put the clams directly on the medium-high-heat side of the grill.

Put the butter, wine, garlic, and paprika in a 12- to 14-inch heavy ovenproof frying pan and place the pan on the medium-low-heat side of the grill.

Cover the grill and cook the clams, checking occasionally, until they open fully, 6 to 8 minutes. Transfer the clams as they open to the pan (discard any that do not open after 8 minutes). Remove the pan from grill. Squeeze the lemon halves over the clams and sprinkle with the parsley.

── **Westport Rivers Vineyard** ──

The Russell family, founders of Westport Rivers Vineyard & Winery, admit that what they've devoted themselves to doing in New England since 1986 is out of the ordinary: "It is emboldened madness to grow grapes for wine in Massachusetts." Yet that madness, along with sustainable practices and involvement by the whole family, has produced some award-winning wines such as the sparkling Brut Cuvée "RJR" (Gold Medal, 1990, the American Wine Society) the Blanc de Blancs (Gold Medal, 2012 Grand Harvest Awards), as well as a respected Grace Chardonnay, Pinot Noir, Riesling, Gruner Veltliner, and more.

Carol Russell, from a family of upstate New York vintners, and Bob Russell, retired from his job as a high-tech metallurgist, wanted to foster something that spoke not only to their heritage but also to preserving the agricultural land surrounding them. Their 400 acres on the southern coast of Massachusetts is testament to both, with sons Rob (who plants and tends the vines) and Bill (who makes the wine) carrying the Westport torch of inspired vineyard madness into the future.

Grilled Sweet Potatoes with Molasses Glaze

★ JOHN "DOC" WILLOUGHBY   SERVES 4 TO 6 AS A SIDE DISH

4 medium sweet potatoes
(about 2 lb.)

Kosher salt

2 Tbs. molasses

2 Tbs. fresh orange juice

1 Tbs. unsalted butter, melted

Pinch allspice

Freshly ground black pepper

Vegetable oil, for the grill rack

Molasses and orange juice combine to make a deep-bright blend that, with a touch of allspice, brings a more complex flavor to sweet potatoes.

Peel the potatoes and cut into ½-inch-thick slices. Transfer to a 3-quart pot, cover by 1 inch with cold water, and add 1 tsp. salt. Bring to a simmer, partially covered, then simmer until just tender. They should give with some resistance when pierced with a fork, 8 to 10 minutes. Remove the potatoes as they are done, and drain.

In a medium bowl, whisk the molasses, orange juice, butter, allspice, ½ tsp. salt, and ¼ tsp. pepper.

Prepare a gas or charcoal grill for medium heat. Oil the grill rack and arrange potatoes on grill and cook, flipping once, until grill marks appear on both sides, 3 to 4 minutes total. Brush the tops with some of the molasses mixture, turn over and cook 30 seconds. Brush the second sides with the molasses mixture, turn over, and cook for 30 seconds more. Transfer the potatoes to a serving platter and season to taste with salt.

━━ Orr's Farm ━━

Andrew Orr had barely graduated from high school when he bought the Westport, Massachusetts, farm he'd been working on for the past three years. With a passion for growing, mentored by farmer Jim Wood, who was about to retire and sell his 13-acre, 107-year-old farm to the Westport Land Conservation Trust, Orr worked out a deal with Wood to buy it himself (with conservation easements in place to keep the land agricultural). Now the young farmer (who, even as a kid, had grown strawberries) grows everything from apples and ground cherries to Asian greens, herbs, eggs, and raises pastured turkeys.

One of the country's new generation of farmers, Andrew Orr was also among the youngest, and his efforts to keep farmland growing and to raise a wide range of produce to keep the land healthy has made people take notice—the *Today* show featured him when he made Wood's farm his own.

Grilled Bluefish with Smoky Chouriço Relish

★ CHRIS SCHLESINGER

SERVES 6

FOR THE SMOKY CHOURIÇO RELISH

1 lb. chouriço, cut in half lengthwise

½ cup diced tomatoes

⅓ cup chopped fresh parsley

¼ cup extra-virgin olive oil

1 Tbs. minced garlic (2 large cloves)

1 large lemon, finely grated to yield 1 Tbs. zest; squeezed to yield 2 Tbs. juice

1 tsp. cumin seeds, lightly toasted

Kosher salt and freshly ground black pepper

FOR THE BLUEFISH

Six 6-oz. bluefish fillets with skin on

Kosher salt and freshly ground black pepper

2 Tbs. vegetable oil

A salute to coastal Massachusetts' vibrant Portuguese community, Schlesinger's bluefish incorporates fresh Portuguese chouriço (housemade at The Back Eddy), which is as spicy as the Mexican version but less crumbly.

MAKE THE RELISH

Prepare a charcoal or gas grill fire for direct grilling over medium-low heat (300° to 325°F). Grill the chouriço until browned and cooked through, 3 to 4 minutes per side. Transfer to a cutting board and cut into small pieces. Transfer to a medium bowl and add the tomatoes, parsley, olive oil, garlic, lemon zest and juice, and cumin seeds. Toss to mix and season to taste with salt and pepper.

COOK THE FISH

Season the fish fillets with salt and pepper and rub them on both sides with the vegetable oil.

Put the fillets skin side up on the grill and cover them with foil. Cook until golden brown (10 to 12 minutes), remove the foil, and flip the fillets with a spatula. Cook the fish until completely opaque throughout, about 5 minutes more.

Remove the fillets from the grill, place them on a platter, and serve them with the smoky chouriço relish.

"These chickens are happy because they're in the grass, they're free-range. They give you happy eggs."

—Jacques Pépin

WILTON, CT

Three of Connecticut's culinary stars—Tim LaBant, Bill Taibe, and the world-renowned Jacques Pépin—know that ingredients never taste better than when they're gathered straight from the source. It's the principle they cook by in their restaurants and home kitchens every day. Inspired by Wilton's Millstone Farm's just-laid eggs, just-picked herbs and greens, heritage hogs and chickens, and honey scooped from the hive, the feast this trio cooks up couldn't be more farm fresh.

FEAST FAVORITES

Scrambled Eggs with Tomatoes and Herbs

JACQUES PÉPIN

Slow-Roasted Pork Shoulder with Salsa Verde

BILL TAIBE, leFarm and The Whelk

Mixed Greens with Fennel-Parmesan Fritters & Bacon-Buttermilk Dressing

TIM LABANT, The Schoolhouse at Cannondale

Strawberry & Honey Buckle with Marsala Ice Cream

TIM LABANT

Scrambled Eggs with Tomatoes and Herbs

★ JACQUES PÉPIN   SERVES 4 TO 6

2 Tbs. olive oil

1 tsp. unsalted butter

2 whole scallions, minced (about 3 Tbs.)

1 large tomato (8 oz.), peeled, seeded, coarsely chopped, and blotted dry (about 1 cup)

½ tsp. kosher salt

6 large eggs

Freshly ground black pepper

2 Tbs. sour cream

¼ cup chopped fresh herbs (a mixture of parsley, chervil, tarragon, and chives), plus more for garnish

4 to 6 medium bibb or butter lettuce leaves

Sour cream takes the place of milk or cream in these fresh-from-the-farm scrambled eggs, lively with herbs and served on smooth butter-lettuce leaves.

In a 10- to 12-inch frying pan, preferably nonstick, heat 1 Tbs. of the olive oil and the butter until the foam from the butter subsides. Add the scallions and cook, stirring, until tender, about 30 to 45 seconds. Add the chopped tomatoes and ¼ tsp. salt and cook, stirring, until they are starting to render their juice but are still firm, about 1 minute. Transfer to a small bowl and set aside.

Wipe the frying pan clean. Heat the remaining 1 Tbs. oil in the pan over medium heat. Meanwhile, beat the eggs with the remaining ¼ tsp. salt and the pepper in a medium bowl. When the oil is shimmering hot, add the egg mixture and stir with a whisk until the mixture is beginning to set but is still a little wet. Whisk in the sour cream and herbs and cook just until the eggs are softly set. Fold in the tomato mixture and remove from the heat.

Arrange the lettuce leaves on a platter. Spoon the egg mixture into the lettuce leaves, and serve warm or at room temperature. Sprinkle with a few extra herbs, if desired.

Slow-Roasted Pork Shoulder with Salsa Verde

★ BILL TAIBE

SERVES 8 TO 10

FOR THE PORK

Kosher salt

1½ cups dark brown sugar

1 large onion, halved

1 large clove garlic, smashed, or 6 spring garlic tops, coarsely chopped

4 Tbs. fennel seed

4 Tbs. black peppercorns

1 tsp. juniper berries, cracked

6-to 7-lb. bone-in pork shoulder with skin

FOR THE SALSA VERDE

2 bunches scallions (about 12 to 14), trimmed

1½ cups extra-virgin olive oil

⅔ cup fresh lemon juice

½ cup coarsely chopped pickled ramps with ½ cup pickled ramp liquid

1 tsp. Aleppo pepper flakes

1 tsp. soy sauce

1 tsp. Asian fish sauce

Kosher salt

1 cup chopped fresh parsley or dill (or combination of both)

16 cups (10 ounces) mixed greens, for serving

For Taibe's salsa verde, he introduces the garlicky flavor of pickled spring ramps (along with their briny pickling liquid), and the heat of Aleppo pepper flakes, which are milder than traditional red pepper. Fish sauce and soy sauce give this South American sauce a taste of Southeast Asia.

BRINE THE PORK

In an 8- to 10-quart pot, combine 5 quarts of cold water, 2 cups salt, the brown sugar, onion, garlic, fennel seed, peppercorns, and juniper berries. Bring the mixture to a boil, then remove the pot from the heat and let cool completely. Once the brine has cooled, add the pork, cover, and refrigerate for 12 to 24 hours.

MAKE THE SALSA VERDE

Thinly slice the whites and green tops of the scallions, and reserve them separately.

Heat ¼ cup of the oil in a 10- to 12-inch frying pan over medium heat. Add the scallion whites and sauté until just softened, 3 to 5 minutes. Remove the pan from the heat and stir in the scallion greens. Transfer all of the scallions to a medium bowl and stir in the remaining 1¼ cups oil, the lemon juice, pickled ramps with liquid, Aleppo pepper flakes, soy sauce, and fish sauce until well blended. Taste and add salt if needed. Cover and chill for 12 to 24 hours.

ROAST THE PORK

Remove the pork from the brine. Place, skin side up, on a rack in a roasting pan and let stand at room temperature for 1 to 2 hours.

Position an oven rack in the middle of the oven and preheat the oven to 300°F. Roast the pork, uncovered, until the meat is easily pierced with a sharp knife (or fork) and a meat thermometer inserted into the center (not touching bone) registers 180°F, about 6 hours. If the skin darkens too quickly before roasting time is complete, tent the pork with foil. →

PORK FAT

Keep leftover pork fat to cook other ingredients (such as potatoes) in later. Store the fat in an airtight container in the refrigerator; it will last for weeks.

Transfer the pork to a cutting board and let rest for 45 minutes. Just before serving, stir the fresh herbs into the salsa verde. Slice the pork and serve over the greens with the salsa verde sauce alongside.

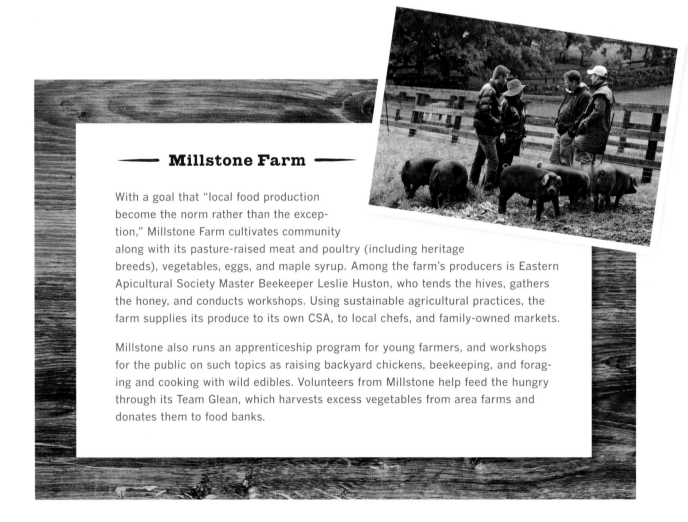

⎯ Millstone Farm ⎯

With a goal that "local food production become the norm rather than the exception," Millstone Farm cultivates community along with its pasture-raised meat and poultry (including heritage breeds), vegetables, eggs, and maple syrup. Among the farm's producers is Eastern Apicultural Society Master Beekeeper Leslie Huston, who tends the hives, gathers the honey, and conducts workshops. Using sustainable agricultural practices, the farm supplies its produce to its own CSA, to local chefs, and family-owned markets.

Millstone also runs an apprenticeship program for young farmers, and workshops for the public on such topics as raising backyard chickens, beekeeping, and foraging and cooking with wild edibles. Volunteers from Millstone help feed the hungry through its Team Glean, which harvests excess vegetables from area farms and donates them to food banks.

Mixed Greens with Fennel-Parmesan Fritters & Bacon-Buttermilk Dressing

★ TIM LABANT   SERVES 6

FOR THE DRESSING

½ cup buttermilk, well-shaken

½ cup mayonnaise

1 medium clove garlic, minced and mashed to a paste with a pinch of salt

1 small whole scallion, trimmed and finely chopped

Kosher salt and freshly ground black pepper

3 slices thick-cut bacon (5 oz.), cut crosswise ¼ inch thick and cooked until crisp

FOR THE FRITTERS AND THE SALAD

Kosher salt

1 large fennel bulb, trimmed (fronds reserved), cored, and coarsely grated on a box grater (about 4 cups)

2 cups coarse fresh breadcrumbs

3 oz. Parmigiano-Reggiano, finely ground in a food processor (about ¾ cup)

2 large eggs, lightly beaten

2 medium cloves garlic, finely chopped

Freshly ground black pepper

½ cup olive oil, plus more as needed

6 oz. mixed salad greens (6 cups packed)

Crisp, cheesy fritters made with grated fennel add a crunchy contrast to a green salad; the dressing contributes a little smoky flavor thanks to the bacon.

MAKE THE DRESSING

In a medium bowl, whisk together the buttermilk, mayonnaise, garlic paste, scallions, ½ tsp. salt, and ½ tsp. pepper. Crumble the bacon and whisk it in. Cover and chill for at least 1 hour and up to 2 days.

MAKE THE FRITTERS AND ASSEMBLE THE SALAD

Bring 5 cups of water to a boil in a 3-quart saucepan. Add 1 tsp. salt and the fennel and cook for 2 minutes. Drain in a fine-mesh strainer and rinse under cold running water until cool. Press out as much water as possible from the fennel, and then transfer to a paper-towel-lined plate. Pat dry with more paper towels.

In a large bowl, gently mix the fennel with the breadcrumbs, Parmigiano, eggs, garlic, and ¼ tsp. pepper.

Heat the oil in a 12-inch cast-iron or nonstick skillet over medium heat until shimmering hot. Using your hands, form a heaping tablespoonful of the fennel mixture into a patty about ½ inch thick. Add it to the skillet and repeat to make 3 more patties, adding them to the skillet as you form them. Cook, turning once, until golden and crisp, 2 to 3 minutes. Transfer to a paper-towel-lined plate to drain. Repeat, in batches, with the remaining fennel mixture, adding more oil as needed.

In a large bowl, toss the greens with just enough of the dressing to lightly coat. Divide among six plates, top with the fritters, and then drizzle with some of the dressing. Garnish with some of the reserved fennel fronds and serve immediately with the remaining dressing on the side, if you like.

"I love using fennel because a lot of people don't think it's supersexy!" —Tim LeBant

Strawberry & Honey Buckle with Marsala Ice Cream

★ TIM LABANT   SERVES 8

Cooking spray

FOR THE STRAWBERRIES

3 cups chopped fresh
   strawberries

1 Tbs. sugar

Zest from ½ lemon

⅛ tsp. kosher salt

¼ cup fresh anise hyssop leaves
   or mint leaves, finely chopped

FOR THE CRUMB TOPPING

½ cup all-purpose flour

⅓ cup packed dark brown sugar

¼ tsp. kosher salt

2 oz. (4 Tbs.) cold unsalted butter,
   cut into small pieces

FOR THE CAKE

4 oz. (8 Tbs.) unsalted butter,
   softened

¾ cup granulated sugar

1 cup all-purpose flour

1½ tsp. baking powder

¼ tsp. kosher salt

1 large egg

½ tsp. vanilla extract

½ cup whole milk

GARNISH

½ cup mild honey

½ cup prepared granola

ACCOMPANIMENT

Marsala Ice Cream
   (see the recipe)

Almost any fruit can be used in this recipe, along with any herb you like. Leftover strawberries are really delicious with yogurt and granola or over ice cream.

Position a rack in the center of the oven and heat the oven to 375°F. Spray the insides of eight 8-oz. mason jars with cooking spray and place the jars in a baking dish or roasting pan.

PREPARE THE STRAWBERRIES

In a medium bowl, combine the strawberries, sugar, lemon zest, salt, and anise hyssop. Toss to combine and set aside.

MAKE THE TOPPING

In a medium bowl, combine the flour, brown sugar, and ¼ tsp. salt. Using your fingers or a pastry blender, blend in the cold butter until the mixture resembles coarse meal. Refrigerate until needed.

MAKE THE CAKE

In the bowl of a stand mixer fitted with a paddle attachment, beat the butter and sugar until light and fluffy. Meanwhile, in a medium bowl, whisk together the flour, baking powder, and salt. Add the egg to the butter and sugar, followed by the vanilla, mixing until combined. Add the dry ingredients in three batches, alternating with the milk and beginning and ending with the dry ingredients.

Spoon 3 Tbs. of the batter into each prepared mason jar. Top the batter with 2 Tbs. of the strawberries mixture (you will have some left over), and top the strawberries with 2 Tbs. of the crumb topping (you will have a little left over), mashing some together to form large clumps.

Bake until the tops are just starting to brown and the edges begin to pull away from the sides of the jar, rotating the pan halfway through, about 45 to 55 minutes.

Remove from the oven and allow to cool slightly, then drizzle each with about 1 Tbs. of honey and top with a tablespoon of granola. Serve with the Marsala Ice Cream.

marsala ice cream

YIELDS 1 QUART

6 large egg yolks

1 cup whole milk

⅔ cup sugar

Kosher salt

1½ cups heavy cream

½ cup sweet Marsala

This ice cream will be soft, so be sure to freeze it until hardened after removing it from the ice cream machine.

In a medium bowl, gently beat the egg yolks and set aside. In a large saucepan, combine the milk, sugar, and a pinch of salt. Bring to a boil and remove the pan from the heat.

In a steady stream, pour half of the milk mixture into the egg yolks, whisking constantly to prevent the eggs from curdling.

Pour the egg mixture back into the saucepan and cook over low heat, stirring constantly and scraping the bottom with a silicone spatula until the custard thickens slightly (it should be thick enough to coat the spatula and hold a line drawn through it with a finger), 4 to 8 minutes. Don't let the sauce overheat or boil, or it will curdle. Immediately strain the custard into a clean bowl. Stir in the cream and Marsala. Cover and refrigerate until completely chilled, at least 8 hours or up to overnight.

Freeze the mixture in an ice cream maker according to the manufacturer's instructions. Transfer the just-churned ice cream to an airtight container, and freeze until hardened, at least 4 hours and up to 2 weeks.

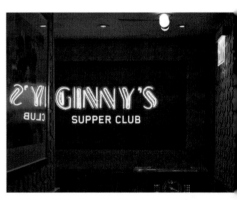

HARLEM, N.Y.C.

This feast flows like great jazz, when downtown chef Jonathan Waxman, of restaurant Barbuto, heads uptown to Harlem to cook with Marcus Samuelsson at Ginny's Supper Club, where music and food harmonize nightly. Just down the road from Samuelsson's restaurant is the 125th Street Farmers Market, where favas, peas, asparagus, greens, and herbs inspire the chefs to bring spring to their dishes. While Waxman waxes Italian with gnocchi and a hearty rack of lamb, Samuelsson draws on the southern and Caribbean influences in Harlem with spicy jerk trout.

FEAST FAVORITES

Gnocchi with Fava Beans, Peas, and Asparagus

JONATHAN WAXMAN, Barbuto

Jerk Trout with Green Goddess Dressing

MARCUS SAMUELSSON, Red Rooster Harlem/Ginny's Supper Club

Rack of Lamb with Kale Salad and Potatoes

JONATHAN WAXMAN

Gnocchi with Fava Beans, Peas, and Asparagus

★ JONATHAN WAXMAN   SERVES 4 AS A FIRST COURSE OR SIDE DISH

FOR THE GNOCCHI

3 russet potatoes (about
   1¾ lb.)

2 cloves garlic, chopped

1 sprig fresh rosemary

Kosher salt

12 oz. (1½ cups) all-purpose
   flour, plus more for dusting

1 large egg

½ Tbs. olive oil, plus more for
   the cooked gnocchi

FOR THE VEGETABLES

½ cup peas, fresh or frozen

½ cup fava beans, fresh or
   frozen

6 medium spears asparagus,
   ends trimmed

8 sugar snap pea pods, strings
   removed

2 Tbs. extra-virgin olive oil

1 oz. (2 Tbs.) unsalted butter

Kosher salt and freshly ground
   black pepper

FOR SERVING

1 oz. Parmigiano-Reggiano,
   finely grated (½ cup with a
   rasp grater)

The freshness of the spring quartet of vegetables (including both English peas and snap peas) in Waxman's dish keeps the hefty gnocchi light. This recipe makes more gnocchi than you will need, but the remainder can be frozen for later use.

MAKE THE GNOCCHI

Put the potatoes in a 4- to 5-quart saucepan and cover with 1 inch of cool water. Add the garlic, rosemary, and 1 Tbs. salt. Bring to a boil, and then reduce the heat and simmer over medium heat. Cook until the potatoes are tender when pierced with a fork, about 45 minutes. Remove the cooked potatoes from the water and let them cool slightly.

When the potatoes are just cool enough to handle, peel them and force them through a ricer onto a clean work surface, making a well in the center. Add half of the flour, the egg, and the olive oil to the well and knead until well combined. Continue to add the flour in ¼-cup increments until it is absorbed into the egg-oil mixture and a dough begins to form. You may not need all the flour. When the dough is still moist but no longer sticky, form it into a ball. Cut the ball into quarters with a sharp knife. Wrap three of the pieces in plastic and put them in the refrigerator.

Roll the remaining piece of dough on the work surface into a ½-inch-thick rope, dusting with flour as needed to prevent it from sticking. Using a sharp knife, cut the rope into ¾-inch pieces and transfer them to a lightly floured baking sheet. Repeat this process with the remaining dough pieces.

Set aside about 60 gnocchi for four servings, and refrigerate, covered with plastic wrap, on baking sheets until needed. Freeze the remainder for another use on baking sheets for about 45 minutes, or until the gnocchi pieces are firmly frozen. Transfer the gnocchi to a freezer bag and store for future use.

BLANCH THE VEGETABLES

Bring a 7- to 8-quart pot of well-salted water to a boil over high heat. Have ready a large bowl of ice water. Prepare a large paper-towel-lined plate and set aside. Add the peas to the boiling water and cook until

CHOOSING FAVA BEANS

Grown in large, fleshy pods that have a thick, cottony lining, and encased in a pale, fairly thick skin, favas become thicker and more bitter as they grow larger. Look for small to medium fava beans, which are more tender and sweeter than the starchier larger beans.

tender, about 3 minutes. Remove from the water with a slotted spoon and immediately plunge into the ice-water bath. When cool, transfer the peas to the paper-towel-lined plate.

Add the fava beans to the boiling water and cook until just tender, about 5 minutes. Remove from the water with a slotted spoon and immediately plunge into the ice-water bath. When cool, drain the favas and peel the outer skin. Place the beans on the plate with the peas.

Add the asparagus to the boiling water and cook until tender, 3 to 5 minutes. Remove from the water with a slotted spoon and immediately plunge into the ice-water bath. When cool, transfer the asparagus to the paper-towel-lined plate.

Repeat this process with the sugar snap peas and drain on the plate with the asparagus. Cut the asparagus and snap peas into ¾-inch diagonal pieces. Set aside. Continue to boil the blanching water.

COOK THE GNOCCHI

Set aside a large bowl for the cooked gnocchi. Drop as many gnocchi into the boiling water used to blanch the vegetables as will fit without crowding. When gnocchi rises to the top, continue cooking for another 1 to 1½ minutes. Remove from the water with a slotted spoon, place in the reserved bowl, drizzle with ½ tsp. of olive oil, and gently mix with a rubber spatula to prevent sticking. Repeat this procedure with the remaining gnocchi.

COOK THE VEGETABLES

Heat the olive oil and butter in a 12-inch skillet over medium heat until shimmering. Add the cooked gnocchi and cook, stirring occasionally, until they just begin to brown, 3 to 4 minutes. Add the peas, fava beans, asparagus, sugar snap peas, ½ tsp. salt, and ½ tsp. pepper and cook until the vegetables are just warmed through, about 2 minutes. Add some of the pasta water to the pan if the mixture seems dry. Adjust the seasoning if necessary.

TO SERVE

Spoon the mixture into shallow serving bowls and top with the cheese.

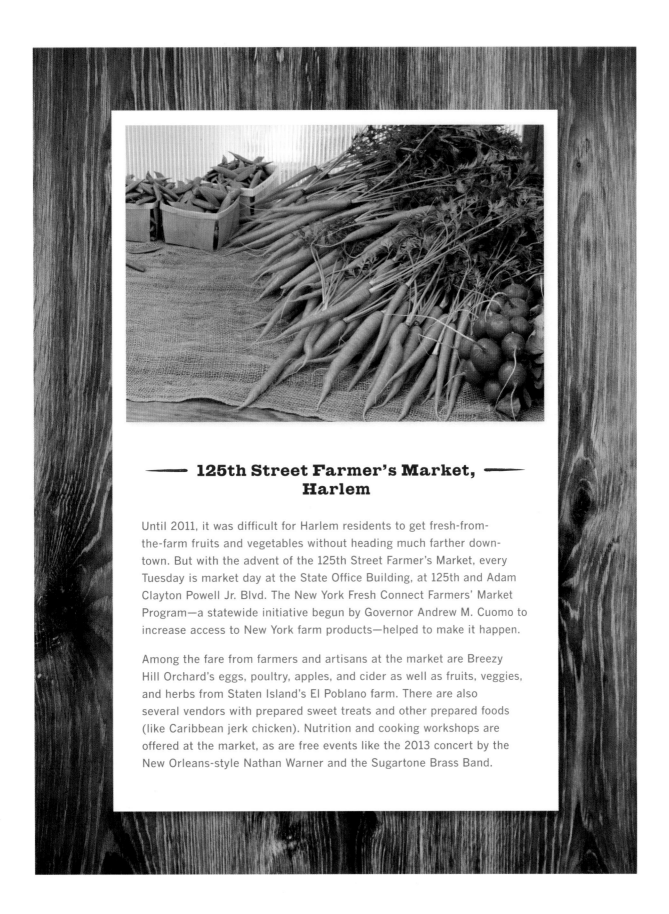

━━ 125th Street Farmer's Market, ━━
Harlem

Until 2011, it was difficult for Harlem residents to get fresh-from-the-farm fruits and vegetables without heading much farther down-town. But with the advent of the 125th Street Farmer's Market, every Tuesday is market day at the State Office Building, at 125th and Adam Clayton Powell Jr. Blvd. The New York Fresh Connect Farmers' Market Program—a statewide initiative begun by Governor Andrew M. Cuomo to increase access to New York farm products—helped to make it happen.

Among the fare from farmers and artisans at the market are Breezy Hill Orchard's eggs, poultry, apples, and cider as well as fruits, veggies, and herbs from Staten Island's El Poblano farm. There are also several vendors with prepared sweet treats and other prepared foods (like Caribbean jerk chicken). Nutrition and cooking workshops are offered at the market, as are free events like the 2013 concert by the New Orleans-style Nathan Warner and the Sugartone Brass Band.

Jerk Trout with Green Goddess Dressing

★ MARCUS SAMUELSSON   SERVES 6

**FOR THE JERK GLAZE
(MAKES ABOUT ¾ CUP)**

3 whole scallions, trimmed and finely chopped

2 cloves garlic, finely chopped

1 habanero or Scotch bonnet pepper, ribs and seeds removed and finely chopped

3 Tbs. molasses

2 Tbs. brown sugar

2 Tbs. soy sauce

1½ Tbs. extra-virgin olive oil

1½ Tbs. rum

½ Tbs. fresh lemon juice

½ Tbs. dried thyme

½ tsp. ground allspice

½ tsp. ground cinnamon

⅛ tsp. ground nutmeg

Kosher salt and freshly ground black pepper

**FOR THE GREEN GODDESS DRESSING
(MAKES ABOUT 1¾ CUPS)**

½ cup coarsely chopped fresh flat leaf parsley

½ cup coarsely chopped fresh dill

¼ cup sliced fresh chives

2 anchovies, patted dry

2 Tbs. Champagne vinegar

1½ cups extra-virgin olive oil

Kosher salt and freshly ground black pepper

FOR THE TROUT

Six 5-oz. trout fillets with skin, pin bones removed

Kosher salt and freshly ground black pepper

Olive oil, for brushing pan

Hot, hot, hot is the rule for a jerk spice rub, and this glaze, with its habanero or Scotch bonnet pepper, does the job. Cool green goddess dressing balances the heat. Chef Samuelsson also likes to garnish the trout with a poached quail's egg and fresh vegetable salad (as pictured). We have simplified the recipe for the home cook.

MAKE THE JERK GLAZE

Combine the scallions, garlic, chile pepper, molasses, brown sugar, soy sauce, olive oil, rum, lemon juice, thyme, allspice, cinnamon, nutmeg, ½ tsp. salt, and ¼ tsp. pepper in the bowl of a food processor and process until blended. Pour the mixture into a small bowl and set aside. Clean the food processor bowl.

MAKE THE GREEN GODDESS DRESSING

Put the parsley, dill, chives, anchovies, and vinegar in the bowl of the food processor and process until finely chopped. With the machine running, slowly pour in the oil and process until blended. Pour the dressing into a bowl and season to taste with salt and pepper. Set aside.

GLAZE AND ROAST THE TROUT

Position a rack in the center of the oven and heat the oven to 450°F.

Dry each piece of trout with a paper towel and season with salt and pepper. Line a rimmed baking sheet with foil. Brush the foil with olive oil and place the trout on the baking sheet, skin side down. Generously brush the trout with the jerk glaze and roast for 6 to 8 minutes, or until the flesh is tender and opaque.

TO SERVE

Spoon about ¼ cup of the dressing onto each of six serving plates, and top each with a piece of trout.

Rack of Lamb with Kale Salad and Potatoes

★ JONATHAN WAXMAN SERVES 4

½ lb. fingerling potatoes

3 Tbs. olive oil

Kosher salt and freshly ground black pepper

1½ Tbs. Dijon mustard

1½ Tbs. fresh lemon juice

¼ cup minced shallot

4 cups julienned fresh kale leaves

One 8-bone rack of lamb (about 1¼ lb.)

1 Tbs. butter

Every morsel of succulent lamb is used in Waxman's recipe—he doesn't French the rack (trimming the meat and fat between the bones).

Position an oven rack in the center of the oven, and heat the oven to 400°F. Toss the potatoes with ½ Tbs. of the oil and season with salt and pepper. Put the potatoes in a small roasting pan and roast in the oven until golden brown and tender, 15 to 20 minutes. Let the potatoes cool and then cut on an angle into ¼-inch-thick slices.

Combine the mustard, lemon juice, shallot, and 1½ Tbs. of olive oil in a large bowl and season with salt to taste. Add the kale and toss to mix. Let stand at room temperature for 10 minutes.

Cut 8 chops from the rack of lamb; do not French. Season the lamb chops generously with salt and pepper. In a large, heavy, cast-iron skillet melt the butter with the remaining 1 Tbs. of the olive oil over medium-high heat until shimmering. Add the lamb chops, in batches, and cook until browned and crispy and medium rare (130° to 135°F), 3 to 5 minutes a side. Transfer the lamb to a platter.

In the same skillet, heat the fingerling potatoes, stirring often, for about 3 minutes or until heated through. Add the potatoes to the kale and toss to mix and coat. Serve the kale salad over the lamb chops.

> *"For dessert, the sun sets between Manhattan skyscrapers, a delicious end to a cross-culinary adventure."*
> —Pete Evans

MIDTOWN MANHATTAN, N.Y.C.

In the heart of New York City, culinary cultures mix it up with three chefs who are worldly-wise in the kitchen. Anita Lo, an alum of television series *Iron Chef* and *Top Chef Masters,* and owner of West Village restaurant Anissa, blends Asian and Lebanese flavors in a steak tartare.

Andy Ricker brings his wide knowledge of Thai cooking to the succulent duck dish pet pha lo. Host Pete Evans taps into a Malaysian classic with fresh crab laksa. A trip to New York's quintessential specialty food shop Kalustyan's gives the chefs all the exotic spices they could imagine.

FEAST FAVORITES

Steak Tartare with Cinnamon, Allspice, and Sesame-Tofu Sauce
ANITA LO, Annisa

Soft-Shell Crab Laksa
PETE EVANS, HOST

Pet Pha Lo (Stewed Duck) with Chile Dipping Sauce
ANDY RICKER, Pok Pok (N.Y.C. and Portland, OR)

Steak Tartare with Cinnamon, Allspice, and Sesame-Tofu Sauce

★ ANITA LO   SERVES 4 AS A FIRST COURSE

FOR THE TARTARE

8 oz. fresh beef tenderloin

¼ cup bulgur

3 Tbs. finely chopped red onion

1½ Tbs. extra-virgin olive oil

1 Tbs. fresh lemon juice

⅛ tsp. ground cinnamon

⅛ tsp. ground allspice

Kosher salt and freshly ground
   pepper to taste

FOR THE TOFU SAUCE

7 oz. silken tofu

2 Tbs. Chinese sesame paste

1 small clove garlic, minced
   and mashed into a paste

Finely grated zest of 1 lemon

2 Tbs. fresh lemon juice

Kosher salt and freshly ground
   black pepper

GARNISHES

1 cup canola oil, for frying

One 8-inch round spring roll
   wrapper

Kosher salt

1 scallion, green parts only, cut
   into 2-inch thin strips

Cayenne pepper

Chinese red chili oil

Extra-virgin olive oil

For the best steak tartare, use beef tenderloin (the tail end) and always hand-chop the meat. It should never be ground. Lo adds a bit of bulgur for even more texture.

MAKE THE TARTARE

Freeze the beef for 30 minutes in order to make it firm and easier to dice. Using a sharp knife, dice the meat into ⅛-inch cubes. Place in a large bowl, cover with plastic wrap, and refrigerate until ready to use.

Cook the bulgur according to the package directions. Rinse with cold water, drain well, and set aside until room temperature.

In a small bowl, mix the red onion, olive oil, lemon juice, cinnamon, and allspice. Set aside.

MAKE THE TOFU SAUCE

Combine the tofu, sesame paste, garlic, lemon zest and juice, 1 tsp. salt, and ¼ tsp. of pepper in a blender. Purée until the mixture is smooth, scraping down the sides of the blender as necessary, 3 to 5 minutes. Pour the sauce into a bowl and season to taste with salt and pepper.

MAKE THE GARNISH

Heat the canola oil in a 2-quart saucepan over medium heat until it is shimmering hot. Using a pair of kitchen scissors, cut the spring roll wrapper into 8 triangles by first cutting it in half, and then each half into quarters.

Fry the triangles one or two at a time until they just crisp, about 30 seconds. Using a slotted spoon, transfer the triangles to paper towels to drain. Season lightly with salt.

TO ASSEMBLE AND SERVE

Add the bulgur and red onion mixture to the beef, and fold the mixture together with a wooden spoon until well combined.

Divide the tartare mixture into four equal portions, about 3 oz. each. Position a 2 x 2½-inch rectangular (or similar) mold on a plate and place a portion of the tartare into it, pressing down and spreading the mixture

into the mold evenly with the back of a teaspoon, or simply scoop a portion into a mound on the plate.

Top the tartare with several strips of scallion. Spoon about ¼ cup of the tofu sauce on the plate next to the tartare. Lightly dust the tofu sauce with the cayenne pepper. Put a few drops of chili oil and extra-virgin olive oil on the plate next to the tofu sauce. Place two of the crispy spring roll wrapper triangles on the plate. Repeat with the remaining tartare on three more plates.

Soft-Shell Crab Laksa

★ PETE EVANS

SERVES 6

FOR THE CRISP-FRIED SHALLOTS

1 large shallot, cut crosswise into thin rings

⅓ cup all-purpose flour

1 cup vegetable oil

FOR THE LAKSA

6 oz. bean thread vermicelli noodles

6 medium cloves garlic

3 oz. (about 2) long red chiles, stemmed, seeded, and coarsely chopped

¼ cup chopped fresh cilantro stems

2 lemongrass stems, white part only, thinly sliced

5 (single) fresh kaffir lime leaves, thinly sliced

1 tsp. ground turmeric

Three 14-oz. cans unsweetened coconut milk

2 Tbs. grated palm sugar (jaggery)

½ tsp. tamarind concentrate, optional

6 cleaned soft-shell crabs (about 3½ oz. each after cleaning)

3 Tbs. fish sauce

3 Tbs. fresh lime juice

¼ napa cabbage, finely shredded (2 cups)

4 oz. firm tofu, diced into ¾-inch cubes

Laksa is a traditional spicy noodle dish of Southeast Asia (especially Malaysia). It's chile-rich and bright with lemongrass and kaffir lime leaves, but has plenty of coconut milk to temper the heat. In Evans's version with crab, it becomes a one-bowl meal.

FRY THE SHALLOTS

Put the shallot in a wide bowl, add the flour, and toss to coat, separating the rings as you go. Put them in a sieve over the bowl and shake off the excess flour.

Heat the oil in an 8-inch skillet over medium-high heat until shimmering hot. Add the shallots in batches and fry until crisp. Transfer to paper towels to drain as fried. Set aside.

MAKE THE LAKSA

Soak the noodles in a bowl of cold water for 30 minutes to soften.

Meanwhile, in the bowl of a food processor, process the garlic, chiles, cilantro stems, lemongrass, lime leaves, and turmeric with 2 Tbs. water to make a paste, or pound using a mortar and pestle.

Bring the coconut milk to a boil in a 6-quart pot over medium-high heat, stirring occasionally. Add the spice paste, palm sugar, and tamarind, if using, and stir well until the sugar is dissolved. Add the crab, bring back to a boil, then turn off the heat and let it sit for 5 minutes, or until the crab is just cooked through (an instant-read thermometer inserted in the center of the crab should read 145°F).

Add the fish sauce, lime juice, cabbage, and tofu. Turn the heat back on to medium high and cook for 1 minute, then remove from the heat.

COOKING SOFT-SHELL CRAB

Because they're so juicy, soft-shell crabs can splatter during cooking, so stand back or use a splatter screen over your pan.

TO SERVE

1 handful of bean sprouts, trimmed

1 cup fresh basil leaves

1 cup fresh mint leaves

1 cup fresh cilantro leaves

3 limes, halved

TO SERVE

Divide the noodles and crab among four bowls, spoon over the sauce and garnish with the bean sprouts, herb leaves, and crisp-fried shallots. Serve with the lime halves.

Pet Pha Lo (Stewed Duck) with Chile Dipping Sauce

★ ANDY RICKER   SERVES 4

FOR THE PET PHA LO

1 oz. dried shiitake mushrooms

1 cup Thai thin white soy sauce

Scant ⅓ cup Thai black soy sauce

2 oz. rock sugar or granulated sugar (scant ⅓ cup)

4 stalks lemongrass, bottoms and top 4 inches trimmed, outer layers discarded, and smashed with side of a chef's knife

1 stalk celery, trimmed and cut into 3-inch lengths

1 oz. ginger, peeled and thinly sliced

1 Tbs. cilantro stems, smashed with side of a chef's knife

1 Tbs. black peppercorns

1½-inch piece cinnamon

1 star anise

4 bay leaves

2 lb. duck legs (about 4), skin removed; rinsed in cold water

FOR THE CHILE DIPPING SAUCE (MAKES ABOUT 1 CUP)

3 oz. mild fresh yellow chiles, such as Fresnos, gueros, or Hungarian wax peppers, seeded and cut crosswise into ¼-inch slices (about 1 cup)

1 tsp. thinly sliced cilantro stems

Kosher salt

5 cloves garlic, peeled and halved lengthwise

1 cup white vinegar

2 Tbs. granulated sugar

Thai soy sauces have a flavor that's distinct from Chinese or Japanese sauces, and are an important element in this slow-cooked duck dish. Chef Ricker uses both thin or "white" soy sauce, which is light and transparent, and the thicker, stronger black variety.

MAKE THE PET PHA LO

Put the shiitakes in a medium heatproof bowl and cover with 2 cups of boiling water. Soak until very soft, about 1 hour. Using a slotted spoon, transfer the mushrooms to a 5½- to 6-quart pot. Slowly pour the soaking liquid through a fine sieve into the pot, leaving any silt in the bowl.

Add 5 cups water, both soy sauces, the sugar, lemongrass, celery, ginger, cilantro, peppercorns, cinnamon, star anise, and bay leaves to the pot and stir to blend. Add the duck legs and bring to a simmer. Lower the heat, cover, and cook until the meat comes off the bone very easily with a tug of tongs but isn't dry or falling off the bone, about 2 hours.

MAKE THE CHILE DIPPING SAUCE

Have ready a medium bowl of ice and water. Bring a 3-quart pot of salted water to a boil. Add the chiles and cook just until they have lost their raw texture and flavor, about 45 seconds. Drain, transfer to the ice water to cool completely, and drain again.

Pound the cilantro stems and 1½ tsp. salt in a mortar and pestle to a coarse paste, about 15 seconds. Add the garlic and pound until blended, and then add the chiles and pound until you have a coarse paste, about 1 minute. Stir in the vinegar and sugar until the sugar is fully dissolved. (Alternatively, you can make the sauce in a food processor.) Transfer the sauce to a medium bowl and set aside.

Remove the duck legs from the pot. Reserve the cooking liquid, if desired, for another use. Serve the duck legs with the dipping sauce.

> *"You have to beat the [bleep] out of the pork! Then it will be thin enough to cook quickly."*
>
> **—Gabrielle Hamilton**

LITTLE ITALY, N.Y.C.

It doesn't get more Italian than this New York neighborhood, where chefs Gabrielle Hamilton (Prune) and Marco Canora (Hearth) gather a crew at restaurant Sophia's of Little Italy for a down-home feast. But before they start cooking they pay calls on the area's mainstay butcher and cheese and meat shops—Pino's Prime Meats and Di Palo's Fine Foods—for juicy pork chops and artisanal mortadella and salami. Canora and Hamilton have made reputations for their homey, laid-back Greenwich Village restaurants with a focus on the neighborhood and on irreverent takes on the classics—they shine in this intimate Italian meal.

FEAST FAVORITES

Di Palo's Antipasto Salad
PETE EVANS, HOST

Fresh Pappardelle with Peas, Butter, and Parmigiano-Reggiano
MARCO CANORA, Hearth, Terroir, and Terroir East

Mushroom Medley in Parchment with Rosemary and Gremolata
MARCO CANORA

Pork Chop Milanese with Belgian Endive and Treviso Salad
GABRIELLE HAMILTON, Prune

—— Di Palo's Fine Foods ——

For four generations, the Di Palo family has kept New Yorkers stocked with Italian cheeses, cured meats, and a pantry's worth of other find Italian products from its Little Italy location. Founded as a latteria (dairy store) in 1910 by Savino Di Palo, after he'd immigrated to the United States from the Basilicata region of Italy, with a more full-service shop opened by his daughter Concetta in 1925, Di Palo's Fine Foods is now in the hands of siblings Luigi (everybody calls him "Lou"), Marie, and Salvatore, and fifth-generation member, Sam.

On Lou's frequent trips to Italy, he's always discovering something new. He has formed bonds with farmers and producers in all 20 regions of the country and brings back cheeses and meats that are hard to find anywhere else. Stroll the shop and you'll see Lagrein (a wine-flavored cheese), Pecorino Toscano Stagionato, Caciocavallo from Basilicata, and homemade burrata; meats like speck from Alto Adige and salame Abruzzese, as well as Italian pastas, rice, olive oil from Sicily, and acacia honey from Prunotto, in the Piedmont.

Di Palo's Antipasto Salad

★ PETE EVANS   SERVES 6 TO 8

½ lb. dried salami, such as cacciatorini, casing removed, cut into ½-inch dice (about 1 cup)

½ lb. mortadella, casing removed, cut into ½-inch dice (about 1½ cups)

½ small head radicchio, cored and cut into bite-size pieces (about 2 cups)

5 marinated artichoke hearts, preferably with stem on, halved lengthwise

One 12-oz. jar roasted red peppers, drained and cut into bite-size pieces

6 oz. Castelvetrano or Cerignola olives, pitted (about 1 cup)

1 Tbs. capers, drained

⅓ cup lightly packed fresh flat-leaf parsley leaves

¼ cup lightly packed fresh basil, smaller leaves only

¼ cup pine nuts, toasted

1½ Tbs. fresh oregano leaves, lightly chopped

¼ cup extra-virgin olive oil

2 Tbs. red-wine vinegar

Kosher salt and freshly ground pepper

Using the highest quality ingredients is key to this salad. Pete used Di Palo's cacciatorini (hunter's sausage) that's rich with red wine and garlic. A tip for easily removing a dried salami casing: soak the links in warm water for 10 minutes to loosen the casing. Sicilian Castelvetrano olives are a good choice for their meaty, fruity, buttery flavor.

In a large bowl, combine the salami, mortadella, radicchio, artichoke hearts, red peppers, olives, capers, parsley, basil, pine nuts, and oregano. Toss to combine.

In a small bowl, whisk the oil and vinegar together and season to taste with salt and pepper. Toss the mixture with enough dressing to coat and serve.

Fresh Pappardelle with Peas, Butter, and Parmigiano-Reggiano

★ MARCO CANORA SERVES 4 TO 6

Kosher salt

1½ oz. prosciutto rind

2 cups lower-salt chicken broth

¼ cup extra-virgin olive oil

1 oz. (2 Tbs.) unsalted butter

1 medium leek, dark-green top removed, light part halved lengthwise, cleaned, and thinly sliced (1 cup)

6 medium scallions, trimmed and thinly sliced (1 cup)

Freshly ground black pepper

1 lb. fresh pappardelle pasta

1 cup English peas, fresh or frozen

1 oz. finely grated Parmigiano-Reggiano (1 cup using a rasp grater), plus more for serving

¼ cup chopped fresh flat-leaf parsley

A prosciutto rind infuses the broth with flavor—ask your deli person to cut you a chunk of rind from the back of the prosciutto. For the broth, you can also use a combination of chicken, beef, and turkey, as Chef Canora did, to add a touch of smokiness to the dish.

Bring a large pot of well-salted water to a boil.

Combine the prosciutto rind and chicken broth in a 3-quart saucepan and bring to a boil. Reduce to a simmer, cover, and cook for 10 minutes to infuse the broth. Let the rind steep until you're ready to use the broth.

Meanwhile, in a 12-inch skillet heat the olive oil and 1 Tbs. of the butter over medium heat until the foaming subsides. Add the leek and scallions, season with ½ tsp. salt and ¼ tsp. pepper, and cook, stirring often, until softened, about 8 minutes.

Add the pasta to the boiling water and cook, stirring occasionally, until 1 minute under al dente.

Remove the prosciutto rind and add the broth to the skillet with the leeks and scallions. Bring to a boil and reduce by half, about 7 minutes. Stir in the peas and the remaining 1 Tbs. butter.

Using tongs, carefully transfer the pasta to the skillet, reserving the pasta water. Add the Parmigiano and parsley and toss well to combine. Season to taste with salt and pepper, adding some pasta water to loosen if necessary. Serve immediately with additional cheese.

Mushroom Medley in Parchment with Rosemary and Gremolata

★ MARCO CANORA SERVES 6 (2 SERVINGS PER PACKET)

1 oz. dried porcini mushrooms

1 cup lightly packed coarsely chopped fresh flat-leaf parsley leaves

2 large lemons, 1 grated to yield 1 Tbs. zest and squeezed to yield 3 Tbs. juice, the other thinly sliced

5 medium cloves garlic

Kosher salt

¼ cup olive oil

2¼ lb. mixed mushrooms, such as cremini, maitake, shiitake, white button, and oyster, cleaned, trimmed, and quartered (about 4 cups)

2 sprigs fresh rosemary, lightly crushed

Freshly ground black pepper

"Gremolata," says Chef Canora, "is like Italian MSG. It makes everything taste good." It's important, he adds, to chop the gremolata blend of parsley, lemon zest, and garlic cloves together, not separately. Ready-made parchment packets are available in the supermarket's foil-and-plastic-wrap aisle.

In a large bowl, cover the porcini with 2 cups boiling water. Let sit until the mushrooms are softened, about 20 minutes. Transfer the mushrooms with a slotted spoon to a clean bowl. Strain the soaking liquid through a coffee filter or paper towel and reserve the liquid.

Heat the oven to 375°F.

Combine the parsley, lemon zest, and 3 of the garlic cloves and chop to combine. Add a pinch of salt and mix well. Transfer the gremolata to a small bowl and set aside.

Heat 2 Tbs. of the oil in a 12-inch skillet over medium-high heat. Cook half the mushrooms (including the porcinis) with 1 of the garlic cloves smashed with the side of a chef's knife and 1 sprig rosemary. Season to taste with salt and pepper and cook, stirring occasionally, until the mushrooms soften and become golden, about 5 minutes. Transfer to a large bowl and repeat with the remaining oil, mushrooms, garlic, and rosemary.

Pour ¼ cup of the reserved porcini soaking liquid into the hot pan. Using a wooden spatula, scrape up all the browned bits and simmer the liquid until reduced by half. Pour into the bowl with the cooked mushrooms and toss. (The remaining soaking liquid can be frozen and reserved for another use.)

Fold three 12 x 17-inch pieces of parchment in half crosswise. Cut each piece into a half-oval as large as the paper allows, leaving the folded side uncut. Unfold the parchment ovals and distribute the mushroom mixture equally in the center of one side of each oval. Evenly drizzle the

lemon juice and sprinkle the gremolata among the three packets. Season to taste with salt and pepper. Fold the parchment over the mushrooms and crimp and pleat the edges to seal tightly, starting at one corner of the fold and working your way to the other end, making sure the seals are tight. You can do this up to 2 hours ahead.

Put the packets on two baking sheets and bake until the gremolata is fragrant and the mushrooms are warmed through, about 5 minutes. Slice open the packets and serve family style with sliced lemon.

— Pino's Prime Meats —

Back in the day, Greenwich Village was a collection of small dairy shops, mom-and-pop grocers, and butcher shops where customers and owners knew each other well. Pino Prime Meats is one of those—a century-old butcher shop with a hand-lettered sign and sawdust on the floor (nightly shavings from the butcher block) that offers well-marbled aged beef and Parma ham and tender pork and lamb, in cuts from steaks to chops to roasts to anything a customer needs (or that Pino suggests, and he does; it's the advice people come for). It defies the odds of the neighborhood. In 2014, Pino's was awarded the Greenwich Village Historic Preservation award. Born and raised on an Italian farm, Pino comes from generations who practiced his craft. "Grandparents, great-grandparents, cousins—even the women! They're all butchers," says son Leo, who, with his brother Sal, carries on the tradition. The tiny butcher shop may be colorful—it has been shot for scenes in films *The Godfather, Part II* and *The Pope of Greenwich Village*—but it's for Pino, Leo, and Sal that customers come.

Pork Chop Milanese with Belgian Endive and Treviso Salad

★ GABRIELLE HAMILTON   SERVES 4

2 heads Belgian endive (about 10 oz. total), trimmed and very thinly sliced lengthwise (2½ cups)

1 head Treviso or radicchio, very thinly sliced lengthwise (about 3 cups)

2 medium cloves garlic, grated

4 small oil-packed anchovy fillets, patted dry and finely chopped (about 1 Tbs.)

¼ cup fresh lemon juice

Kosher salt and freshly ground black pepper

Four 6- to 7-oz. boneless pork chops

½ cup all-purpose flour

2 eggs, beaten

2 cups panko

¼ cup olive oil

Chef Hamilton's pork chops were bone-in and cooked in clarified butter. However, it's often difficult to thoroughly cook the meat close to the bone in bone-in chops, so we swapped them for boneless versions. We also used olive oil instead of clarified butter to cook the pork. It doesn't produce a chop that's as rich and juicy as Chef Hamilton's, but it's a leaner alternative.

In a large bowl of ice water, combine the endive and Treviso and let sit for at least 20 minutes and up to 2 hours to remove some of the bitterness.

Using your hands, lift the lettuces out of the ice bath and lightly shake to dry. The leaves should remain slightly wet. Transfer to a large bowl and add the garlic, anchovy, and lemon juice. Using your hands, toss to combine and massage the garlic, anchovy, and lemon juice into the endive and Treviso. Season to taste with salt and pepper and refrigerate, covered, until ready to serve.

Place each pork chop between two pieces of plastic wrap and pound with a meat mallet until ¼ inch thick. Season both sides of the pork chops generously with salt and pepper.

Put the flour, eggs, and panko in each of three separate pie plates or bowls large enough to hold one of the pork chops. Dredge each pork chop in the flour, then the egg, then the panko, lightly pressing on the panko to adhere. Transfer to a plate and refrigerate for 15 minutes.

Meanwhile, heat half of the oil in a 12-inch heavy-duty skillet over medium heat until shimmering. Carefully add 2 of the pork chops to the skillet and cook until golden on both sides and just cooked through, about 5 minutes total. Repeat with the remaining oil and chops. Let the chops rest for about 5 minutes.

Top each pork chop with a mound of endive and Treviso salad. Serve immediately.

> *"Pork is so versatile. I'm slightly obsessed with the pig."*
> —April Bloomfield

STATEN ISLAND, NY

Staten Island may not be New York City's best-known borough, but it has a rich history, including the landmark Casa Belvedere, home to the Italian Cultural Foundation. Before they hop a ferry to the island, chefs Pete, Seamus Mullen, and April Bloomfield gather fresh produce at Brooklyn Grange, a groundbreaking (literally) urban farm, and select artisanally produced pork and duck at Dickson's Farmstand Meats. Then it's a boat ride past the Statue of Liberty to cook up a feast at the Belvedere that speaks to the city's Italian and Spanish influences, and to the glory of a New York spring. Award-winning English chef Bloomfield carries on the celebration of pork she conducts daily at her Spotted Pig restaurant, while Chef Mullen, an expert in Spanish cuisine, assembles a dynamite paella and a piquant salad featuring the Basque sheep's-milk cheese Idiazábal. A treat for all the senses, the feast is accompanied by the Belevedere's spectacular view of New York Harbor.

FEAST FAVORITES

Duck Confit Salad with Raisins, Fennel, and Apple
PETE EVANS, HOST

Brooklyn Grange Salad with Pickled Eggs and Idiazábal
SEAMUS MULLEN, Tertulia

Roasted Coppa-Wrapped Pork Loin
APRIL BLOOMFIELD, The Spotted Pig, The Breslin, and The John Dory

---

Minty Spring Vegetable Sauté
APRIL BLOOMFIELD

Duck Confit Salad with Raisins, Fennel, and Apple

★ PETE EVANS

SERVES 6 TO 8

2 Tbs. whole-grain mustard

2 Tbs. white balsamic vinegar

1 Tbs. honey

1 Tbs. fresh thyme leaves

⅓ cup extra-virgin olive oil

Kosher salt and freshly ground black pepper

Five 7- to 8-oz. confit duck legs

6 oz. (6 cups) hearty mixed greens, such as mustard greens, escarole, frisée, and romaine

1 small (about 10 oz.) fennel bulb, trimmed, cored and thinly sliced

1 small Granny Smith apple, cored and thinly sliced

2 cups fresh flat-leaf parsley leaves

⅓ cup golden raisins

¼ cup sunflower seeds, toasted

To keep the duck legs extra moist, Chef Evans adds a bit of chicken or duck stock to the baking sheet, but just enough so that the skin still gets beautifully crisp. (To make homemade duck confit, see finecooking.com/recipes/ homemade-duck-confit.aspx) Thyme and duck just go together, says Evans, who liberally adds the fresh leaves, along with parsley, to this hearty salad.

Position a rack in the upper third of the oven and heat the oven to 450°F.

In a medium bowl, combine the mustard, vinegar, honey, and thyme. While whisking, add the oil in a slow, steady stream until emulsified. Season to taste with salt and pepper.

Put the duck legs skin side up on a large rimmed baking sheet. Bake until the skin is deep golden brown and crisp and the duck is heated through, rotating the sheet halfway through baking, about 25 minutes. Set aside to cool.

When cool enough to handle, remove the skin and slice into ¼-inch-thick strips; set aside. Shred the meat into bite-size pieces and transfer to a large bowl. Season to taste with salt and pepper. Transfer half of the meat to a small bowl and set aside.

Add the greens, fennel, apple, parsley, raisins, and sunflower seeds to the duck in the large bowl. Add the dressing and toss gently to coat. Season to taste with salt and pepper. Transfer to a large serving platter and top with the reserved shredded duck meat and the duck skin.

Brooklyn Grange Salad with Pickled Eggs and Idiazábel

★ SEAMUS MULLEN   SERVES 6

FOR THE EGGS

6 large eggs

1 quart homemade or store-bought pickled beets

FOR THE SALAD

4 oz. (1 cup) honey-glazed pecans

1 tsp. ground Aleppo pepper

6 salt-cured anchovy fillets in olive oil, drained and finely chopped

1 Tbs. finely chopped preserved lemons

½ cup plus 2 tsp. extra-virgin olive oil

1 small clove garlic

Kosher salt and freshly ground black pepper

1 Tbs. Dijon mustard

⅓ cup sherry vinegar

5 oz. (about 5 cups) mixed baby greens

1 oz. (about 1 cup) mixed herbs and edible flowers, thinly sliced

1 medium kohlrabi or 9 oz. broccoli stems, peeled, cut in half, and thinly sliced, preferably on a mandolin

5 medium radishes thinly sliced, preferably on a mandolin

Flaky sea salt, such as Maldon®

1 oz. (about 1 cup) finely grated Idiazábal or manchego

¼ oz. (about 2 Tbs.) freshly grated horseradish (optional)

1 Tbs. finely grated lemon zest (from 1 large)

Chef Mullen's salad calls for preserved lemons, an essential ingredient in Moroccan dishes that is simple to prepare and have on hand.

FOR THE EGGS

Bring a 2-quart pot of water to a boil over high heat. Gently add the eggs, reduce the heat to a simmer, and cook for 7 minutes. Drain immediately and run under cold water until the eggs have cooled completely. Peel and transfer to a medium bowl.

Carefully pour enough of the pickling liquid over the eggs to cover, leaving the beets behind in the jar. Cover the eggs with plastic wrap and refrigerate for at least 24 hours.

FOR THE SALAD

Position a rack in the center of the oven and heat the oven to 300°F.

Spread the honey-glazed pecans on a parchment-lined rimmed baking sheet. Mist lightly with water and sprinkle the Aleppo pepper evenly over the nuts, gently pressing the pepper to adhere. Bake until aromatic and warmed through, about 5 minutes. Set aside to cool.

In a mortar and pestle, combine the anchovies, preserved lemons, 2 tsp. of the oil, garlic, and a generous pinch of kosher salt and pepper. Pound the mixture to a paste, transfer to a medium bowl, and whisk in the mustard and the vinegar. In a slow, steady stream, whisk in the remaining ½ cup oil. Season to taste with kosher salt and pepper.

In a large bowl, combine the greens, herbs and flowers, kohlrabi, radishes, and pecans and season to taste with kosher salt and pepper. Toss to lightly coat with the vinaigrette and gently transfer to a large serving platter.

Remove the pickled eggs from the brine and gently pat dry. Halve the eggs lengthwise and sprinkle the cut sides with the flaky sea salt. Arrange the eggs over the greens. Evenly sprinkle the cheese, horse-radish, if using, and lemon zest over the salad and serve.

Roasted Coppa-Wrapped Pork Loin

★ APRIL BLOOMFIELD   SERVES 4 TO 6

10 oz. medium scallions (about 2 bunches), trimmed

20 dried bay leaves

4 medium cloves garlic, finely grated

5 oz. (⅔ cup) lard, softened

Kosher salt

¾ lb. sweet capocollo, thinly sliced

2 lb. boneless pork loin

Freshly ground black pepper

¼ cup olive oil

1 cup red wine

Fresh mint leaves, for garnish

Lemon wedges, for serving

Flaky sea salt, such as Maldon

Capocollo is another name for the Italian dry-cured meat known as coppa, which comes from the neck and shoulder of the pig. Chef Bloomfield appreciates the gentle aroma and delicate flavor of authentic coppa di Parma. You can substitute olive oil (or puréed pork back fat, as Bloomfield did for the Feast) for lard to rub the loin if you prefer.

Cut the scallions (mainly whites) to the width of the pork loin and set aside. In a spice grinder, grind the bay leaves down to a fine powder. Coarsely chop the remaining scallion greens and transfer to a food processor along with 1 tsp. of the ground bay leaves, the garlic, lard, and 1 tsp. salt. Pulse until smooth and set aside.

Arrange the capocollo slices on a sheet of plastic wrap large enough to go around the roast, overlapping each slice so it covers about half of the slice below it and next to it, leaving no gaps; you want to form a "sheet" of capocollo that's as wide as the roast and long enough to go around it. Arrange extra slices of capocollo extending from the center of the sides to cover the ends of the roast as well.

With a small offset spatula or a butter knife, carefully spread the lard mixture all over the capocollo slices. Season the roast all over with salt and pepper. Position the roast at the center of the capocollo and, using the plastic, wrap the capocollo up and around the sides of the pork, tucking in the side slices to cover the ends of the roast. Wrap the roast in the plastic and refrigerate for at least 30 minutes and up to 24 hours.

Position a rack in the center of the oven and heat the oven to 450°F.

Unwrap the roast and tie with butcher's twine at 1-inch intervals both lengthwise and crosswise to keep the capocollo secured. Heat the oil in a 12-inch nonstick skillet over medium-high heat until shimmering. Sear the roast on all sides, including the ends, until golden brown, about 3 minutes per side.   →

Arrange the reserved scallion whites in an even row in the center of a medium roasting pan to create a bed for the roast; place the roast on top of the whites. Pour the accumulated juices from the skillet around the roast.

Transfer to the oven and roast for 10 minutes to crisp the capocollo. Reduce the oven temperature to 325°F; after 15 minutes, add the wine and continue to cook until an instant-read thermometer inserted in the center of the roast registers 140°F, 25 to 30 minutes.

Transfer the roast to a cutting board and let sit, tented with foil, for 10 minutes. Thinly slice the roast and transfer the slices to a serving platter. Top with the roasted scallions, pan juices, and mint. Serve with lemon wedges and flaky sea salt.

═══ Dickson's Farmstand Meats ═══

"A candy store for carnivores," is how owner Jake Dickson describes his Dickson's Farmstand Meats in New York City's Chelsea Market. At Dickson's, artisanal poultry, beef, pork, and lamb are on offer, as well as house-made charcuterie.

The meat is all sourced from a half-dozen or so farms that are within a 400-mile radius of New York and that put sustainable, organic, and humane ideals into practice. "The farmers not only talk the talk, they walk the walk," says Dickson. From the Sir William Angus farm, in Craryville, New York, for example, one of the oldest breeders of Berkshire pigs in the country, Dickson gets pork plus certified Angus beef and pasture-raised veal. Dickson started his career in corporate marketing, but, drawn to the food business and high-quality meats in particular, he decided to get his hands dirty and do intensive apprenticeships on farms and butcher shops. He opened Dickson's Farmstand Meats in 2009. Dickson's also offers classes, both demos and hands-on, to help those who want to master those tricky cuts.

Brooklyn Grange

Launched in 2010 by a group with a lot of farm know-how and engineering skills, and a goal of sustainable urban farming in mind, Brooklyn Grange is an urban farm operation that grows more than 50,000 pounds of organically cultivated produce on the rooftops of New York. The two buildings used for vegetable farming (one in the Brooklyn Navy Yard and one in Long Island City, Queens) comprise more than 2 acres of "green roof" (specially designed systems of soil, drainage plates, and root barriers). There are also egg-laying hens and 30 hives for honeybees at Brooklyn Grange Bees, a commercial apiary where future beekeepers are trained and honey is harvested. Selling to restaurants, as well as through farmers' markets and a CSA, the Grange also now shares its knowledge with others through its green-roof design and installation team.

Minty Spring Vegetable Sauté

★ APRIL BLOOMFIELD

SERVES 4 TO 6

Kosher salt

3 cups (9½ oz.) sugar snap peas, cleaned

14 oz. (1 bunch) asparagus, cut into 1-inch pieces on the diagonal

1½ cups fresh or frozen peas

1 cup shelled fava beans or edamame or frozen lima beans

6 oz. (about ½ bunch) rainbow chard, stems cut into 1-inch pieces on a diagonal, leaves coarsely chopped

5 cups (5 oz.) baby spinach

2 Tbs. extra-virgin olive oil

1½ oz. (3 Tbs.) unsalted butter, softened

6 oz. (1 bunch) scallions, coarsely chopped

2 medium cloves garlic, minced

Freshly ground black pepper

Flaky sea salt, such as Maldon

Fresh mint leaves, for garnish

Lemon wedges, for serving

This buttery blend of seasonal vegetables can be eaten warm or at room temperature. If fresh favas aren't in season, you can substitute lima beans or shelled edamame.

Bring a large pot of well-salted water to a boil. Prepare an ice water bath and set side. Line a rimmed baking sheet with paper towels and set aside. Blanch the sugar snap peas, asparagus, peas, fava beans (or edamame or lima beans), and chard leaves separately in batches until tender, about 2 minutes each. Blanch the spinach until tender, about 1 minute. Blanch the chard stems until tender, about 6 minutes. As completed, transfer the blanched vegetables to the ice bath with a slotted spoon. Drain the vegetables on the paper towels.

In a 12-inch skillet over medium heat, combine the oil and butter and cook until the butter is lightly browned, about 2 minutes. Add the scallions and garlic, season with ½ tsp. kosher salt and ½ tsp. pepper, and cook, stirring, until softened, about 2 minutes. Add the blanched vegetables and cook, stirring occasionally, until heated through, 5 minutes more. Transfer to a large platter and sprinkle with flaky sea salt and garnish with mint leaves. Serve with lemon wedges.

THE SOUTH

Our second season of *Moveable Feast* found us in Louisiana not once, not twice, but three times. There's that much to experience in the state where Cajun and Creole food join a new style of southern cooking that's perfectly comfortable keeping company with the classics. We went from the streets of New Orleans to the deep Mississippi Delta, meeting farmers and fishermen who take pride in what they raise and how it's cooked. Then we threw feasts that could only be imagined below the Mason-Dixon Line.

The southern cooks who showed us the way have a passion for keeping local flavors alive and getting to know their history. If there's such a thing as the voice of Louisiana cooking, it may well be Poppy Tooker. As producer and host of the weekly NPR show *Louisiana Eats!*, Tooker, a New Orleans native, introduces listeners to the edible life of the place she calls home. With Tooker and Chef Susan Spicer, who set a new standard for New Orleans dining at Herbsaint and Bayona, there was a feast that drew on the tastes of historic New Orleans, Caribbean influences, and the bounty that grew right there at Bartlett Farm, where the meal was held.

Some have called Chef John Folse an evangelist for Louisiana cuisine. He was born, he says, "20 yards from the swamp floor pantry of south Louisiana's Bayou Country," and he's been letting his roots do the talking in his kitchen (and on television and radio) for four decades. Walking the walk with Chef Folse is seafood aficionado and biologist Chef Brian Landry, of restaurant Borgne, who grew up fishing the Gulf waters and eating crawfish boils with his family. For Landry, Gulf seafood is something worth conserving—he joined the Louisiana Seafood Board as an ambassador chef. The result? Landry's buttery speckled trout and Folse's gumbo laced with spicy homemade andouille sausage.

Donald Link, who grew up in Cajun country, and his restaurant Chefpartner Stephen Stryjewski, of Cochon and Pêche, take their feast to a storied Mississippi River plantation, where a crawfish and crab boil is just the start to a delicious lesson in what it's like to roll (and cook) on the river.

"Three hundred years ago in New Orleans, you had several different nations coming together at the same time, bringing their techniques, philosophy, and raw ingredients. It's a great place to cook!" —John Folse

NEW ORLEANS, LA

You can't visit New Orleans without eating a big bowl of gumbo, and when that gumbo is cooked by Chef John Folse—whose knowledge of the area's food history is unparalleled—you know that's going to be one great bowl. Local speckled trout gets the royal treatment from Chef Brian Landry, whose seafood expertise shines a bright light on the new generation of chefs. And Pete gets a lesson in making and smoking andouille sausage (a Cajun classic). To top it off, the feast is held at the Freret-Bultman House, where Tennessee Williams once wrote *The Glass Menagerie*. Now *that's* New Orleans.

FEAST FAVORITES

Louisiana Chicken Liver Paté with Andouille Sausage, Cherrykraut, and Seeded Crackers

PETE EVANS, HOST

Death by Gumbo

JOHN FOLSE, Restaurant R'evolution

Trout en Papillote with Blue Crab Butter

BRIAN LANDRY, Borgne

Coffee, Cinnamon, and Honey Crème Brûlée

JOHN FOLSE

Louisiana Chicken Liver Pâté with Andouille Sausage, Cherrykraut, and Seeded Crackers

★ PETE EVANS   SERVES 8 TO 10 AS AN APPETIZER

FOR THE CRACKERS

1 cup (5½ oz.) golden and/or brown flaxseeds

½ cup total mixed seeds, such as pumpkin, sunflower, sesame

1 tsp. cumin seeds or fennel seeds

½ tsp. fine sea salt, plus more as needed

FOR THE CHICKEN LIVER PÂTÉ

1 lb. chicken livers, drained

Kosher salt and freshly ground black pepper

3 Tbs. duck fat

1 small yellow onion, chopped

1 medium clove garlic, minced

3½ oz. andouille sausage, chopped (about 1 cup)

1 Tbs. chopped fresh flat-leaf parsley →

The secret to cooking chicken livers, or any liver, is to avoid overcooking, which will make them tough. You want the livers to be pink on the inside.

MAKE THE CRACKERS

Put the flaxseeds in a medium bowl and pour in enough water to just cover them. Put the mixed seeds in another medium bowl and pour in enough water to just cover them. Let the seeds soak at room temperature until the flaxseed water appears gelatinous, 8 to 16 hours.

Drain and rinse the mixed seeds and add to the flaxseeds and their liquid. Mix well and drain the entire mixture again, without rinsing, to remove any excess liquid. Transfer the seed mixture back to a bowl and stir in the cumin seeds and salt.

Position a rack in the center of the oven and heat the oven to 200°F. Line a large rimmed baking sheet with a silicone baking mat (parchment and waxed paper will not work here).

With a silicone spatula, thinly spread the seed mixture to the edges of the mat. Bake, flipping the cracker sheet halfway through, until the center feels dry to the touch, 4 to 4½ hours. Remove from the oven and sprinkle with more salt to taste while still warm. When cool, break the cracker sheet into uneven pieces and set aside or store in an airtight container for up to 5 days.

MAKE THE CHICKEN LIVER PÂTÉ

Put the livers on a paper towel and pat dry to remove excess moisture. Season all over with salt and pepper.

Heat 1 Tbs. of the duck fat in a 12-inch skillet over high heat until it's shimmering hot. Working in batches, add the livers to the pan in a single layer and leave undisturbed until browned, about 1 minute. Flip and brown on the other side, about 1 minute more. Transfer to a plate and set aside to cool. Repeat with the remaining livers. →

½ tsp. paprika

½ tsp. fresh thyme leaves

1 small bay leaf

1 Tbs. brandy

1 cup lower-salt chicken broth

FOR THE CHERRYKRAUT

1 lb. packaged, undrained sauerkraut, such as Bubbies® or Boar's Head®

1 small Granny Smith apple, cored and finely diced

2 oz. (½ cup) dried sour cherries, chopped

1 medium clove garlic, minced

⅛ tsp. cumin seeds

⅛ tsp. fennel seeds

To the same pan, add 1 Tbs. of the duck fat, the onion, and garlic. Season generously with salt and pepper. Cook over medium-high heat, stirring often, until golden, 5 minutes. Stir in the sausage and cook until lightly browned, 3 minutes. Stir in the parsley, paprika, thyme, and bay leaf.

Add the brandy and cook, stirring, until almost evaporated, 1 minute. (Careful, the brandy may flare up.)

Remove from the heat and stir in the remaining 1 Tbs. duck fat, the chicken livers, and any juices on the plate. Discard the bay leaf and let the mixture cool slightly, about 10 minutes. Transfer to a food processor and pulse until finely chopped.

Continue pulsing, adding enough chicken broth, 2 Tbs. at a time, until a smooth paste forms. Season to taste with salt and pepper. Transfer the pâté to a medium bowl and cover with plastic wrap. Refrigerate until completely chilled and the flavors have melded, at least 2 hours. Remove from the refrigerator 15 minutes before serving, stir, and adjust seasoning if necessary.

MAKE THE CHERRYKRAUT

Combine all the ingredients in a large bowl. Refrigerate until completely chilled and the flavors have melded, at least 2 hours. Remove from the refrigerator about 15 minutes before serving and toss.

Serve the chicken liver pâté and crackers with the cherrykraut on the side.

— Covey Rise Farms —

More than 50 New Orleans–area restaurants create dishes from the baby greens, radishes, herbs, fingerling potatoes, and up to 150 varieties of other vegetables grown on Covey Rise Farms' 35 acres in Husser, Louisiana. But if you had asked the farm's owner, Sandy Sharp, about becoming a farmer before 2009, he would have thought you were joking. Sharp was a lawyer and a land developer, and a good bit of his 400-acre property was devoted not to growing vegetables but to a preserve for fly fishing; hunting quail, duck, and pheasant; and as a corporate retreat at the Covey Rise Lodge.

Sharp and Jimbo Geisler, who owned the hunting operation on Sharp's land, decided to add a farm and dip into agritourism. Ten planted acres now number 50. Working closely with chefs has helped to make Covey Rise a success. Sharp also launched a community-supported agriculture program and sells at the New Orleans Hollygrove Market. Ducks, eggs, and, Sharp says, "the prettiest hogs around," are raised at sister company Chappapeela Farms.

Death by Gumbo

★ JOHN FOLSE

FOR THE GAME HENS

6 Cornish game hens, 1¼ to 1½ lb. each

Kosher salt and cracked black pepper

2 Tbs. garlic powder

1½ cups cooked white rice

2 Tbs. chopped fresh flat-leaf parsley

1 tsp. gumbo filé powder

1 oz. andouille sausage, cut into twelve ⅛-inch-thick slices

6 raw oysters, shucked

½ cup vegetable oil, plus more as needed

FOR THE GUMBO

2¼ oz. (½ cup) all-purpose flour

1 small yellow onion, cut into ½-inch dice (1 cup)

3 medium celery stalks, cut into ½-inch dice (1 cup)

½ large red bell pepper, cut into ½-inch dice (½ cup)

6 medium cloves garlic, minced (2 Tbs.)

3 oz. white button mushrooms, stemmed and thinly sliced (½ cup)

2½ oz. andouille sausage, cut into ½-inch dice (½ cup)

Gumbo begins with making a roux, a combination of oil and flour that thickens, colors, and flavors the dish. Chef Folse likes to strain his gumbo before serving it, but you can also enjoy it as is—chock-full of vegetables and sausage.

ROAST THE HENS

Position a rack in the center of the oven and heat the oven to 400°F.

Pat the hens dry inside and out. Sprinkle each hen inside and out with ¼ tsp. salt, ¼ tsp. cracked black pepper, and ¼ tsp. garlic powder.

In a small bowl, combine the rice with the parsley, filé powder, ½ tsp. salt, ¼ tsp. pepper, and ¼ tsp. garlic powder. Stuff the cavity of each hen with 1 piece of sausage to plug the neck opening, ¼ cup of the rice mixture, 1 additional slice of sausage, and 1 oyster, pressing each into the rice mixture. Truss the legs of each hen with twine and secure the lower cavity opening with a toothpick to keep the stuffing inside.

Heat the vegetable oil in a 7- to 8-quart Dutch oven over medium-high heat until shimmering hot. Working in batches, sear the hens, breast side down, until deep golden brown, about 5 minutes. Transfer the hens, breast side up, to a lightly oiled roasting pan.

Roast the hens until an instant-read thermometer inserted into the thickest part of a thigh registers 165°F, 25 to 35 minutes. Transfer the hens to a cutting board, tent with foil, and set aside.

MAKE THE GUMBO

Meanwhile, adjust the amount of oil in the Dutch oven to measure ½ cup. Heat the oil over medium-high heat until shimmering hot. Whisk in the flour, stirring constantly and scraping up any caramelized bits from the hens. Cook the roux until it's smooth and a deep chocolatey brown, about 15 minutes.

Add the onion, celery, bell pepper, and minced garlic. Cook until the vegetables begin to soften, about 5 minutes. Stir in the mushrooms and sausage and cook until the mushrooms soften, about 3 minutes. Slowly

1½ quarts lower-salt chicken broth; more as needed

½ tsp. chopped fresh thyme

Kosher salt and cracked black pepper

4 medium scallions, thinly sliced (½ cup)

½ cup chopped fresh flat-leaf parsley; more for garnish

stir in the chicken broth, stirring constantly, until the liquid is the consistency of heavy cream.

Stir in the thyme, bring to a boil, and then reduce the heat to maintain a simmer. Cook, uncovered, stirring occasionally, until reduced by half, about 30 minutes. Season to taste with salt and pepper. Stir in the scallions and parsley, and remove from the heat.

Ladle about ¾ cup of gumbo in a wide, shallow bowl, nestle a hen in the center, and sprinkle with parsley. Serve.

Trout en Papillote with Blue Crab Butter

★ BRIAN LANDRY SERVES 4

FOR THE CRAB BUTTER

2 whole fresh or thawed, frozen gumbo or blue crabs

10½ oz. (1 cup plus 5 Tbs.) unsalted butter

⅛ tsp. paprika

Pinch turmeric

Kosher salt

Freshly ground white pepper or ground cayenne pepper

FOR THE PAPILLOTE

5½ oz. (½ cup plus 2 Tbs.) crab butter

1 medium yellow onion, thinly sliced lengthwise (about 2 cups)

1 small fennel bulb, trimmed, cored, and thinly sliced lengthwise (about 2 cups)

½ cup dry white wine

12 oz. mature spinach, washed and stems removed (about 9 cups)

Kosher salt and freshly ground white pepper

Four 6- to 7-oz. trout fillets, skin on, pin bones removed

1 Tbs. chopped fresh tarragon

1 Tbs. finely grated lemon zest

Vegetable oil

2 cups red and/or yellow grape tomatoes, halved

Lemon wedges, for serving

Cooking fish en papillote—in parchment paper packets—yields moist, tender results with little fuss. The key is a folded seal on the paper packet so the steam can't escape while cooking.

MAKE THE CRAB BUTTER

Bring 1 inch of water to a boil in a 4-quart saucepan fitted with a steamer basket. If using live crabs, hold them with tongs and rinse under cold water to wash off any sand or seaweed. Put the crabs in the saucepan and steam, covered, until the shells are bright red, about 10 minutes.

Remove the crabs from the steamer and let cool. Remove the steamer from the saucepan and wipe out the pan.

Return the crabs to the saucepan, and with a meat mallet or heavy wooden spoon, break up the shells, legs, and claws until some of the meat is exposed. Add ½ lb. of the butter, the paprika, turmeric, ¼ tsp. salt, and a few grinds of white pepper or a pinch of cayenne. Over low heat, melt the butter and bring to a simmer. Cook, occasionally crushing the shells more, until the butter is infused with the crab flavor, about 30 minutes.

Remove from the heat and let sit for 10 minutes. Strain the butter through a fine-mesh strainer into a medium heatproof bowl, pressing on the solids to extract all the liquid. Set the bowl over a larger bowl filled with ice water.

Whisk the butter until it starts to firm up, about 2 minutes. Transfer to a mini food processor and add the remaining 2½ Tbs. butter, cut into ½-inch cubes. Process until smooth and well blended.

Scrape the butter into a small bowl, cover with plastic, and refrigerate until firmly set, about 2 hours. You can make the butter up to 5 days ahead.

MAKE THE PAPILLOTE

Position racks in the upper and lower thirds of the oven and heat the oven to 400°F.

Melt 2 Tbs. of the crab butter in a 12-inch skillet over medium heat. Add the onion and fennel and cook until they begin to caramelize, about

15 minutes. Add the wine and bring to a simmer, scraping up any browned bits on the bottom of the pan, about 2 minutes. Turn the heat up to medium high and fold the spinach into the onion mixture. Cook, stirring occasionally, until the spinach is completely wilted, about 3 minutes. Season to taste with salt and pepper and set aside.

Rinse the trout fillets under cool water. Pat dry with paper towels and place on a baking sheet. Season both sides generously with salt and pepper, and sprinkle the tops of the fillets equally with the tarragon and the lemon zest.

Cut four 15 x 24-inch sheets of parchment. Fold each sheet in half, forming a 15 x 12-inch rectangle. With a pencil, draw a half-heart on each, centering it on the folded edge. Cut out the hearts. (This shape is easier to seal than a rectangle.)

Unfold one of the parchment hearts and arrange on a work surface. Coat the inside with vegetable oil, leaving a 1-inch border.

Place ½ cup of the spinach mixture (without liquid) on one half of the heart near the fold. Place one fillet on top of the spinach. Spread 1 to 2 Tbs. of crab butter on top of the fillet (reserve remaining crab butter for another use). Top with ½ cup of grape tomatoes. Season with a sprinkling of salt and a few grinds of pepper.

Fold the other half of the parchment over and line up the edges. Starting at the top of the heart, fold over about ½ inch of the edge, pressing down to make a crisp crease. Continue working your way around the edge of the packet, making overlapping folds (like pleats), always pressing firmly and creasing the edge so the folds hold. Twist the tip of the heart to finish. If necessary, make a second fold anyplace that doesn't appear tightly sealed. Repeat with the remaining parchment and ingredients.

Transfer the packets to two large rimmed baking sheets and bake until the packets are puffed and fragrant, 10 to 12 minutes.

Place a packet on each plate and slice or tear open the top, folding back the edges of the parchment. Serve immediately, garnished with lemon wedges.

"Wild-caught fresh seafood is such a staple of my diet. I don't know that I could live in a landlocked area!" —Brian Landry

Coffee, Cinnamon, and Honey Crème Brûlée

★ JOHN FOLSE SERVES 6

3 cups heavy cream

1 cup whole milk

¼ cup plus 2 Tbs. granulated sugar

¼ cup honey

1 Tbs. instant coffee

½ tsp. ground cinnamon

¼ tsp. kosher salt

9 large egg yolks

Whipped cream, raspberries, and mint leaves for garnish (optional)

Chef Folse describes this dessert as a cold Café Brûlot, the classic New Orleans drink made with coffee, brandy, citrus peel, and spices that's served flambé style. By far the easiest method of caramelizing sugar on a crème brûlée is with a propane blowtorch. Blowtorches are sold in most hardware and kitchenware stores. Enjoy these desserts as is or topped with whipped cream, raspberries, and fresh mint leaves.

Position a rack in the center of the oven and heat the oven to 300°F. Fill a teakettle with water and bring to a boil. Put six 6-oz. ramekins (about 3 inches in diameter and 1¾ inches deep) in a baking dish that's at least as deep as the ramekins.

In a heavy-duty 3-quart saucepan, whisk together the cream, milk, ¼ cup sugar, honey, instant coffee, cinnamon, and salt. Bring the cream mixture just to a simmer, stirring occasionally, over medium-high heat. (Do not boil.)

Meanwhile, in a large bowl, lightly whisk the egg yolks. Lightly whisk about ½ cup of the cream mixture into the yolk mixture and stir for about 30 seconds; this tempers the yolks. Then gently whisk in the remaining cream, stirring for about 15 seconds to blend. Use a light hand—you don't want to make the mixture frothy or the baked custards will have a foamy-looking surface.

Strain the custard through a fine-mesh strainer into a large measuring cup or heatproof bowl with a spout. Divide the custard equally into the ramekins in the roasting pan. Slowly pour the boiled water into the roasting pan until it reaches about halfway up the sides of the ramekins, being careful not to get water into the custard.

Bake the custard until the edges are set about ⅓ inch in from the sides of the ramekins and the center is slightly jiggly (like Jell-O®), about 1 hour. To test for doneness, reach into the oven with tongs and give one of the ramekins a gentle shake or nudge. If the custard responds with a wave-like motion rather than a slight jiggle, it's not firm enough; bake for another 5 minutes and check again. →

Transfer the ramekins to a wire rack to cool, then refrigerate at least 4 hours and up to 3 days.

When ready to serve, place the ramekins in the freezer for 15 minutes. Remove from the freezer and, working with one custard at a time, top with 1 tsp. of the remaining sugar. You may need to tilt and tap the ramekin to even out the layer of sugar. Wipe any sugar off the rim of the ramekin.

Hold the torch flame 2 to 3 inches from the top of the custard and slowly glide it back and forth over the surface until the sugar melts and turns a deep golden brown. Allow the sugar to cool and harden for a few minutes. Top with whipped cream, raspberries, and mint leaves, if desired, and then serve immediately, before the sugar softens and gets sticky.

——— The Farm at White Oak ———

For chefs John Folse and Rick Tramonto of New Orleans Restaurant R'evolution, it's not enough to buy local produce; they started their own farm. In Gonzales, Louisiana, not far from Folse's White Oak Plantation, a stately Baton Rouge property that hosts catering and special events, he turned land into farmland, raising pigs, chickens, and cows; setting up beehives; and building a smokehouse to cure meats for the restaurant's charcuterie program. The Farm at White Oak was born.

Folse puts his 25-acre farm to work, pampering his heritage-breed animals, including Ossabaw Island, Berkshire, and Large Black hogs; Buff Orpington, Black Australorp, and Buckeye hens; and Wagyu beef cattle. He refurbished an old outbuilding to create "Ole Smokey," to hot- and cold-smoke meats and sausages; and enlisted retired Louisiana State University entomology professor Dr. Dale Pollet to help launch the beehives (which produce White Oak Plantation honey). Now, the R'evolution menu is about as farm-to-table as a chef can get.

"It all started
with my granddad,
watching him cook
for twenty people
and make it so good."
—Donald Link

WEST POINT À LA HACHE, LOUISIANA

There are plenty of fish in the Mississippi Delta, where New Orleans chefs Donald Link and Stephen Stryjewski pick up their bows for a new kind of river adventure. Just 40 miles from the city, at a former plantation built by a sometime-pirate, they catch redfish and then go crabbing in Lake Hermitage, gathering seafood for the next day's Cajun feast. These two should know all about that—they're partners in the award-winning seafood restaurant Pêche. This is a menu that speaks to the best Cajun country has to offer.

FEAST FAVORITES

SoCo Woodland Punch
FOSTER CREPPEL, owner of Woodland Plantation

Boiled Crawfish and Crabs
DONALD LINK, Herbsaint, Cochon, and Pêche

Grilled Oysters with Cajun Compound Butter
STEPHEN STRYJEWSKI, Cochon and Pêche

Grilled Redfish with Onions
STEPHEN STRYJEWSKI

Classic Bread Pudding
DONALD LINK

SoCo Woodland Punch

★ FOSTER CREPPEL   SERVES 6 TO 8

3½ cups pineapple juice

2 cups Southern Comfort®

2 Tbs. maraschino cherry juice, plus cherries for garnish

1½ Tbs. fresh lime juice, plus more to taste

¾ cup club soda

Serving Southern Comfort is in Woodland Plantation's DNA. An image of the stately plantation in West Point à La Hache, Louisiana, has graced the Southern Comfort bottle since 1934, and this is the plantation's signature blend.

In a pitcher, combine the pineapple juice, Southern Comfort, cherry juice, lime juice, and club soda.

Fill six to eight pint glasses with ice and divide the punch among them. Stir, top with a cherry, and serve.

Boiled Crawfish and Crabs

★ DONALD LINK

SERVES 6 AS AN APPETIZER

3 large lemons, halved

2 medium oranges, halved

2 large unpeeled yellow onions, halved

¼ cup (about 12) Chinese dried hot red peppers

2 Tbs. whole cloves

2 Tbs. whole coriander seeds

2 Tbs. mixed peppercorns

2 bay leaves

2 oz. kosher salt (5 Tbs. Diamond Crystal®, 4 Tbs. Morton®)

¼ cup Louisiana hot sauce

2 Tbs. Worcestershire sauce

2 Tbs. dry crawfish boil mixture

2 tsp. Louisiana liquid crawfish boil

12 fresh blue crabs, rinsed clean

1 lb. fresh crawfish, rinsed clean

Live blue crabs and crawfish require cleaning before you cook them. To clean the live crabs, hold each one with tongs and rinse under cold running water, being careful not to get too close to their pincers. To clean crawfish, place them in a large bowl with cool water and stir with a spoon to remove the dirt. Transfer to a colander in small batches and rinse with cool running water until the water runs clear. You can adjust the heat level in the dish by using varying degrees of crawfish boil mixture. If you can't find liquid boil, use more dry boil and hot red pepper to taste.

Bring a 12- to 14-quart pot filled halfway with water to a boil. Add the lemons, oranges, onions, Chinese peppers, cloves, coriander, peppercorns, bay leaves, and salt. Return to a boil and let the flavors meld, about 5 minutes. Add the hot sauce, Worcestershire sauce, and dry and liquid crawfish boil.

Add the crabs, pushing them under the surface of the water with tongs, and boil for 7 minutes. Add the crawfish, stir, and continue to boil for 3 minutes more. Turn the heat off and let the crabs and crawfish rest, undisturbed, until completely cooked through, about 10 minutes.

Remove the shellfish from the broth with tongs and arrange on a large platter. Serve immediately.

BLUE CRABS

Blue crabs shed their shells between April and mid-September, as the waters along the Atlantic and Gulf coasts warm. Fishermen catch the crabs before they shed and keep them in bins of seawater to keep track of their progress. As soon as they molt, they're packed in wet straw, paper, or seaweed and shipped to restaurants and stores.

Grilled Oysters with Cajun Compound Butter

★ STEPHEN STRYJEWSKI   SERVES 6 TO 8 AS AN APPETIZER

8 oz. (1 cup) unsalted butter, softened

1 large lemon, finely grated to yield 1 Tbs. zest, squeezed to yield ¼ cup juice

¼ cup coarsely chopped fresh flat-leaf parsley

1½ Tbs. Louisiana hot sauce, plus more as needed

5 medium cloves garlic, minced

½ tsp. Espelette pepper

Pinch cayenne

Kosher salt and freshly ground pepper

2 dozen large oysters, scrubbed clean

Rock salt, for serving

Lemon wedges, for serving

If you need to store your fresh oysters, says Chef Stryjewski, put them in the refrigerator with a wet towel draped over them so the shells don't dry out. And when the oysters are cooked, you'll want to sop up every last drop of the spicy compound butter, so serve a loaf of good crusty bread toasted on the grill alongside.

Heat a gas or charcoal grill to medium high (400° to 475°F).

In a food processor, pulse together the butter, lemon zest and juice, parsley, hot sauce, garlic, Espelette pepper, and cayenne until well combined. Season to taste with salt, pepper, and additional hot sauce. The compound butter can be made up to 5 days ahead and kept in an airtight container in the refrigerator. Let sit at room temperature for 30 to 40 minutes before using.

Grill the oysters with their rounded sides down, covered, until they open, about 5 minutes. With tongs, carefully remove the oysters from the grill and place on a rimmed baking sheet lined with a kitchen towel. (A towel provides support so the oysters don't tip over and lose their liquor.) Let them cool slightly and then remove the top shell and discard.

Carefully run the edge of a small spoon underneath the oyster meat to release it from the shell. Drop 2 tsp. of the compound butter in each oyster and carefully return to the grill. Cook until the butter is completely melted and slightly bubbling, about 4 minutes.

Transfer the oysters to a wide, shallow platter filled with rock salt, nestling them in the salt for stability. Serve immediately with the lemon wedges.

"Season things a little more than you think you should. A little acid from a lemon goes a long way to brighten flavor." —Stephen Stryjewski

Grilled Redfish with Onions

★ STEPHEN STRYJEWSKI

SERVES 6

Six 8-oz. (approx.) redfish, striped bass, or haddock fillets, skin and scales on, pin bones removed

¼ cup olive oil, plus more for brushing

1 tsp. ground dried red chile flakes

Kosher salt and freshly ground black pepper

4 large cloves garlic, very thinly sliced

2½ lb. (about 3 medium) Vidalia onions, peeled and left whole

2 large lemons, 1 juiced (about ¼ cup), the other cut into wedges

3 Tbs. thinly sliced chives

Coarse sea salt, such as fleur de sel, for serving

¼ cup chopped fresh flat-leaf parsley

OVEN OPTION

As an option, you could also cook the fillets on an oiled rimmed baking sheet in the oven at 475°F for 6 to 8 minutes.

Four cloves of garlic give the fish robust flavor—but feel free to adjust the amount of garlic cloves to taste. For the red chile flakes, you can use either the ready-to-go variety from the market or you can crush your own whole dried red peppers (anything from cayenne to Fresno to red-hot Scotch Bonnets will do).

Prepare a charcoal or gas grill fire for indirect cooking over medium heat (350° to 375°F).

Rinse the fillets and pat dry. Brush the skin side of the fillets lightly with oil. Put the fillets on a large rimmed baking sheet, skin side down, and season with the chile, salt, and pepper. Divide the garlic among the fillets and drizzle each with 1 tsp. of the oil. Let marinate while preparing the onions.

Clean and oil the grill. Lightly oil the onions and place them on the hot side of the grill, turning occasionally until charred on all sides, about 15 minutes. Transfer to the cooler part of the grill and cook until softened and a knife pierced into the center comes out easily, about 30 minutes more.

Transfer to a cutting board. When cool enough to handle, halve the onions lengthwise and thinly slice. Put the onions in a medium bowl and drizzle with half of the lemon juice and season to taste with salt and pepper. Toss with the chives and set aside.

Prepare the grill for direct grilling on medium heat (350° to 375°F). Clean and oil the grill.

Place the fish, skin side down, on the grill. Cover the grill and cook, without disturbing, until just cooked through, about 8 minutes. The flesh should flake easily with a fork.

Using a long metal or fish spatula, transfer each fillet to a serving plate. Garnish each with a sprinkling of coarse sea salt, some parsley, a drizzle of the remaining lemon juice, and 1 tsp. of olive oil. Serve with the grilled onions and lemon wedges.

Classic Bread Pudding

★ DONALD LINK   SERVES 12 TO 16

FOR THE BREAD PUDDING

12 oz. (8 cups) day-old baguette, cut into 1-inch cubes

1 quart heavy cream

1½ cups granulated sugar

8 large eggs

4 large egg yolks

1½ tsp. pure vanilla extract

½ tsp. kosher salt

FOR THE CARAMEL SAUCE

1 cup granulated sugar

1½ tsp. light corn syrup

1 cup heavy cream, at room temperature

1 oz. (2 Tbs.) unsalted butter, softened

Pinch of table salt

FOR ASSEMBLY

Unsalted butter, softened

2 Tbs. granulated sugar

2 Tbs. raw sugar, such as turbinado

½ tsp. ground cinnamon

Coarse sea salt, such as fleur de sel

A drizzle of rich caramel sauce makes bread pudding sing. When making the sauce, sugar can burn easily, so use a heavy-based pot, preferably one that doesn't have a dark interior so that you can monitor the sugar once it begins to color.

MAKE THE BREAD PUDDING

Position a rack in the center of the oven and heat the oven to 325°F.

Spread the bread cubes in a single layer on a large rimmed baking sheet and toast until lightly golden, about 7 minutes. Set aside.

In a large bowl, whisk together the cream, sugar, eggs, yolks, vanilla, and salt. Stir in the bread cubes, pressing down to submerge them in the custard. Let the bread soak for 1 hour at room temperature and up to 4 hours, covered, in the refrigerator, occasionally folding the mixture with a spatula.

MAKE THE CARAMEL SAUCE

Meanwhile, fill a small bowl halfway with water and put a pastry brush in it; this will be used for washing down the sides of the pan to prevent crystallization. Combine the sugar, corn syrup, and ¼ cup water in a heavy-duty 4-quart saucepan. Bring the mixture to a boil over high heat, stirring often, until the sugar dissolves and is clear, about 35 minutes. When sugar crystals begin to form on the sides of the pan, wash them down with the wet pastry brush.

Reduce the heat to maintain a gentle boil. Don't stir at this point, but check frequently until the sugar begins to turn a light honey color around the edges, about 10 minutes, brushing down the sides whenever necessary. Gently swirl the pan to even out the color and prevent the sugar from burning in isolated spots. Continue to cook until the sugar turns a rich red-brown color, about 2 minutes more. (Once the mixture begins to color, it will darken very quickly, so keep an eye on it.) Remove from the heat. →

CLEANING UP

For easy cleaning, soak the pot and utensils used for the caramel sauce in hot water. To loosen any cooked-on sugar, fill the pot with water and set it on the heat.

Carefully stir in the cream with a wooden spoon; the caramel will bubble and steam. Continue to stir until any solidified caramel melts. (If it doesn't, set the pan over medium-low heat and stir gently until the caramel is completely smooth.) Stir in the butter and salt. Let cool to room temperature before serving.

ASSEMBLE

Generously butter a 9 x 13-inch baking dish. In a small bowl, stir together the granulated sugar, raw sugar, and cinnamon.

Choose a roasting pan large enough to accommodate the prepared baking dish with an inch or 2 of space on all sides.

Pour the bread mixture into the prepared baking dish and sprinkle evenly with the cinnamon sugar. Cover the dish with aluminum foil, place in the roasting pan, and transfer to the oven. Pour 1 inch of boiling water around the baking dish and bake until the custard is set, about 30 minutes. Remove the foil and continue baking until the top is crisp, about 20 minutes more.

Remove the bread pudding from the roasting pan and let cool for at least 20 minutes. Serve drizzled with the caramel sauce and sprinkled with coarse sea salt.

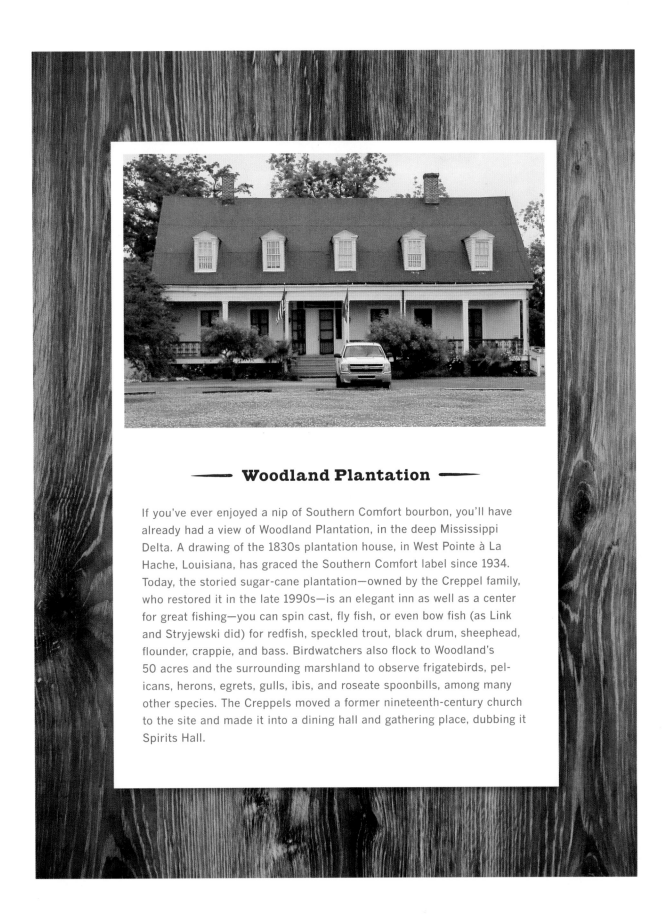

— Woodland Plantation —

If you've ever enjoyed a nip of Southern Comfort bourbon, you'll have already had a view of Woodland Plantation, in the deep Mississippi Delta. A drawing of the 1830s plantation house, in West Pointe à La Hache, Louisiana, has graced the Southern Comfort label since 1934. Today, the storied sugar-cane plantation—owned by the Creppel family, who restored it in the late 1990s—is an elegant inn as well as a center for great fishing—you can spin cast, fly fish, or even bow fish (as Link and Stryjewski did) for redfish, speckled trout, black drum, sheephead, flounder, crappie, and bass. Birdwatchers also flock to Woodland's 50 acres and the surrounding marshland to observe frigatebirds, pelicans, herons, egrets, gulls, ibis, and roseate spoonbills, among many other species. The Creppels moved a former nineteenth-century church to the site and made it into a dining hall and gathering place, dubbing it Spirits Hall.

> "We can tell which season it is by the seafood, from crawfish to crab to oyster."
>
> —Poppy Tooker

COVINGTON, LOUISIANA

For a pop-up farm feast, New Orleans chef, radio host, and cookbook author Poppy Tooker and award-winning chef Susan Spicer take a road trip across Lake Pontchartrain to Bartlett Farm. Along the way they visit Farmhouse Dairy, where artisanal goat's-milk cheeses are crafted. With their Farmhouse ricotta, and the fresh eggs, chicken, and vegetables from Barlett, Pete and the chefs whip up a meal that highlights the flavors of New Orleans, past and present.

FEAST FAVORITES

Madame Begue's Stuffed Eggs

POPPY TOOKER, NPR radio host and author of *Louisiana Eats!: The People, Their Food, and Their Stories*

Swiss Chard Fritters with Whipped Feta and Baby Beets

SUSAN SPICER, Bayona and Mondo

Spicy Chicken with Papaya-Mango Salsa

PETE EVANS, HOST

Madame Begue's Stuffed Eggs

★ POPPY TOOKER   24 EGG HALVES

12 large eggs

4 oz. (8 Tbs.) unsalted butter, softened

½ tsp. Creole or spicy brown mustard

2 Tbs. finely diced carrot

1 scallion, finely chopped (about 1 Tbs.)

Kosher salt

Hot sauce

Paprika

12 thin slices deli ham, cut in half

Poppy Tooker's buttery, spicy stuffed eggs are a tip of the hat to the "late breakfast" served at nineteenth-century New Orleans restaurant Begue's. Proprietor Madame Begue offered but one meal a day, an 11 a.m. breakfast that was popular with dock workers whose early morning shifts ended at that time.

Put the eggs in a large pot, add enough cold water to cover them by 2 inches, and bring to a rolling boil.

Turn off the heat and let the eggs sit, covered, for 8 minutes. Prepare an ice water bath.

Transfer the eggs to the ice water bath to cool completely, 15 minutes.

Peel the eggs, cut in half lengthwise, and remove the yolks. In a medium bowl, using a fork, mash the yolks with the butter and mustard. Stir in the carrot, scallions, 1 tsp. salt, and 1½ tsp. hot sauce, adding more to taste.

Transfer the filling to a quart-size zip-top plastic bag and cut off one of the corners. Pipe the filling into the egg whites. Sprinkle paprika on the filling and top each egg half with one folded slice of ham. Alternatively, gently press one edge of a ham slice into the egg white, then pipe filling on top.

Eggs can be prepared up to 24 hours in advance. Store in the refrigerator, covered with plastic wrap. Return to room temperature before serving.

Swiss Chard Fritters with Whipped Feta and Baby Beets

★ SUSAN SPICER   SERVES 6 TO 8; MAKES ABOUT 2 DOZEN FRITTERS

10 small beets with greens (1¼ lb.), greens reserved and coarsely chopped (about 1 oz.)

Kosher salt and freshly ground white pepper

2 Tbs. balsamic vinegar

6 Tbs. extra-virgin olive oil

8 oz. (1 cup) crumbled feta cheese, at room temperature

10 oz. (1¼ cups) fresh ricotta

2 large lemons, 1 grated to yield 1 Tbs. zest and squeezed to yield 2 Tbs. juice, the other cut into wedges for serving

½ medium fennel bulb, trimmed, cored, and coarsely chopped (about 1 cup)

4 oz. (1 small bunch) Swiss chard, stemmed, leaves coarsely chopped (about 2½ cups)

4¼ oz. (1¼ cups) chickpea flour; more if needed

2 tsp. baking powder

½ tsp. baking soda

3 large eggs

4 medium cloves garlic, minced

3 Tbs. chopped fresh dill, plus sprigs for serving

3 Tbs. chopped fresh mint

½ tsp. ground cinnamon

½ tsp. ground Aleppo pepper

½ tsp. freshly ground nutmeg

Vegetable oil, for frying, about 6 cups

Chef Spicer likes the sweet, rich, "slightly beany" flavor of chickpea flour, which she uses to bind these earthy chard fritters, and the pungent, "not too spicy" taste of Aleppo pepper.

Position a rack in the center of the oven and heat the oven to 425°F.

Put the beets and 2 Tbs. water in an 8 x 8-inch baking dish. Season with salt and pepper, cover with aluminum foil, and roast until tender when pierced with a knife, about 40 minutes. Let the beets sit until cool enough to handle, then peel and slice into quarters. Transfer to a large bowl and toss with the vinegar, 1 Tbs. of the oil, and salt and pepper to taste.

In a food processor, combine the feta, ricotta, lemon juice, and 3 Tbs. of the olive oil. Pulse until combined, then process until the mixture becomes light and fluffy, scraping the sides of the bowl as necessary. Season with salt and pepper.

Heat the remaining 2 Tbs. olive oil in a 12-inch skillet over medium-high heat until shimmering. Add the fennel and season with ½ tsp. salt and ¼ tsp. pepper. Cook, stirring occasionally, until softened, about 6 minutes. Add the beet greens and chard and cook until wilted, about 3 minutes. Remove from the heat and let cool completely.

Transfer a third of the chard mixture to a blender and add the chickpea flour, baking powder, baking soda, eggs, and ⅓ cup water. Blend until combined, scraping down the container as necessary, until the mixture is the consistency of pancake batter. (If the batter is too loose, add chickpea flour to the blender 1 Tbs. at a time and blend until incorporated. If the mixture is too thick, add additional water 1 Tbs. at a time, blending until incorporated.)

Transfer the mixture to a large bowl and fold in the remaining chard mixture, the lemon zest, garlic, chopped dill, mint, cinnamon, Aleppo pepper, nutmeg, 1 tsp. salt, and ¼ tsp. pepper.

→

In a 4- to 5-quart heavy-duty pot fitted with a deep-fry thermometer, heat 2 inches of the vegetable oil over medium-high heat until it reaches 350°F.

Using a tablespoon measure and a small spoon, carefully drop 6 to 8 walnut-size balls of batter into the oil. Fry, turning once, until the fritters float to the surface and turn crisp and light golden brown, 2 to 3 minutes. Transfer to a plate lined with paper towels and sprinkle with additional salt. Continue to fry in batches, being careful not to overcrowd the pot.

To serve, spread the feta mixture on a large platter and top with the fritters, beets, and dill sprigs. Serve with lemon wedges.

"New Orleans is my hometown, and it has everything—great music, great food, great architecture, and friendly, happy people."

—Susan Spicer

—— Bartlett Farm ——

When hurricane Katrina struck southern Louisiana in 2005, it knocked down a bunch of trees on the Covington, Louisiana, property where John Bartlett grew up. And it gave him the idea that he could turn his organic-gardening hobby into a much bigger operation on his own land. The former agriculture student, who'd been turned off by the school's focus on big agribusiness, took to planting pesticide-free lettuces and peppers, eggplant and okra, Asian greens, and all kinds of squash, which now number more than 40 varieties. He got a flock of chickens and raised them free-range, for eggs as well as meat, and he initially called his farm The Garden. And then he started a community-supported agriculture membership.

John's mother, Nancy, who had always been an avid flower gardener, joined in her son's venture and launched expanded cutting gardens; her Blue Stem Flowers business now offers her blooms for sale at farmers' markets, and she has several restaurant clients as well. When they're not working the land or farmers' markets, John and Nancy have hosted farm dinners sponsored by the likes of Outstanding in the Field. And, like all farmers, they persevere through good seasons and bad. One of John's May 2014 Facebook posts gives you a glimpse: "You know you've had too much rain when there are minnows swimming around the puddles in the pasture. Don't worry, we broke out the scuba gear and pulled out some vegetables in time for the Covington market tomorrow. We'll be there rain or shine with a full table."

Spicy Chicken with Papaya-Mango Salsa

★ PETE EVANS

SERVES 4 TO 6

FOR THE CHICKEN

Two 3-lb. whole chickens

1 medium red onion, coarsely chopped

3 medium scallions, coarsely chopped

6 medium cloves garlic, chopped

3 fresh habanero chiles, seeded

¼ cup fresh lime juice

3 Tbs. coconut oil, melted

2 Tbs. tamari

1 Tbs. white-wine vinegar

1 Tbs. honey, preferably raw

1 Tbs. fresh thyme leaves

1 Tbs. smoked paprika

2 tsp. ground allspice

½ tsp. ground cinnamon

¼ tsp. freshly grated nutmeg

Kosher salt and freshly ground black pepper

Canola oil, for the grill and brushing

Lime wedges, for serving

Fresh cilantro and mint leaves, for garnish

With a nod to Caribbean influences in New Orleans, Chef Evans incorporates island flavors in both the spicy marinade and the ripe-fruit salsa. Coconut oil, which is solid at room temperature, needs to be warmed before being added to the marinade—and contributing a deliciously subtle coconut flavor to the poultry.

Working with 1 chicken at a time, put it breast side down on a cutting board. Using a pair of kitchen shears, cut along the length of the backbone on both sides and remove. (Discard or save for stock.)

Flip the chicken, breast side up, and press down with the palm of your hand to flatten. With the shears or a sharp chef's knife, cut the chicken in half lengthwise through the breast bone.

In a food processor, combine the onion, scallions, garlic, habaneros, lime juice, coconut oil, tamari, vinegar, honey, thyme, paprika, allspice, cinnamon, nutmeg, 1½ tsp. salt, and 1½ tsp. pepper. Process to a paste and transfer to a large shallow baking dish, or split among 2 gallon-size zip-top bags. Add the chicken halves and turn to coat. Cover with plastic wrap or seal the bags and refrigerate for at least 2 hours and up to overnight.

Let the chickens sit out at room temperature for 1 hour to lose the chill. Prepare a gas or charcoal grill to medium heat (350° to 375°F). Brush clean and oil the grate with canola oil.

Remove the chickens from the marinade and wipe off the marinade. Brush the chickens all over with canola oil and lightly season with salt. Transfer to the grill and cover, turning occasionally, until an instant-read thermometer inserted in the thickest part of the thigh registers 165°F, about 30 minutes. As the chicken halves are ready, transfer to a large serving platter, cover with foil, and let rest for 5 minutes before serving.

FOR THE PAPAYA-MANGO SALSA

½ medium (about 2 lb.) papaya, peeled, seeded, and diced into ½-inch cubes (about 2½ cups)

1 large (about 1 lb.) mango, peeled and diced into ½-inch cubes (about 1½ cups)

½ medium red onion, finely chopped

1 medium jalapeño, seeded and finely chopped

1 fresh red chile, such as Fresno, seeded and finely chopped

3 Tbs. fresh lime juice

2 Tbs. white-wine vinegar

2 Tbs. chopped fresh cilantro

2 Tbs. chopped fresh mint

Kosher salt

MAKE THE SALSA

Meanwhile, stir together the papaya, mango, onion, jalapeño, red chile, lime juice, vinegar, cilantro, and mint in a large bowl. Season to taste with salt and set aside. The salsa can be made up to 1 day ahead and kept in the refrigerator.

To serve, arrange the chicken on a platter with the lime wedges and sprinkle with cilantro and mint leaves. Pass the salsa on the side.

MIDWEST

For our two midwestern feasts, we explored both city and country to provide a taste of what's cooking in this part of the country. In the past decade or so, Chicago has become a food town known as much for its inventiveness as it has been for its famous deep-dish pizza and hot dogs, thanks to chefs like Stephanie Izard (winner of *Top Chef* Season 4), Gale Gand (*Sweet Dreams*), and the Hearty Boys (*Party Line with the Hearty Boys*) who, through their television shows, have brought their Midwest style to homes across the U.S. Chef Chris Pandel hasn't had a TV show (yet!), but this Illinois native is spreading the love of great food at his Chicago restaurants The Bristol and Balena, to rave reviews.

But that's only one side of the region's story. Midwest farmers are essential to the American food supply. Heartland grains and fields of greens, beans, and hundreds of varieties of vegetables and fruits are a blessing for cooks everywhere. So in celebrating the region, we take you from urban streets, ethnic markets, and restaurants on city rooftops to rural farms and artisans and a meal around a lakeside picnic table, for a snapshot of the best of the Midwest.

"There's a camaraderie among chefs in Chicago. There's no pretense or ego. You can say, 'Show me how you made that.'"

—Chris Pandel

CHICAGO, IL

In the Windy City, chefs like Illinois natives Chris Pandel, of The Bristol, and Stephanie Izard, of Girl & the Goat, are making Chicago's West Loop a mecca for food lovers. The spirit of experimentation is alive here, and Izard and Pandel have made their reputations by bringing it to their cooking time and again. Izard, a *Top Chef* alum with a taste for Asian style, and Pandel, a devotée of nose-to-tail cooking, rely on local specialty shops like Joong Boo Market, for a raft of Asian ingredients, and Nichols Farm & Orchard for just-picked berries, greens, and much more. With visits to market and farm accomplished, Izard and Pandel throw a Korean family-style barbecue (with Italian touches) on "the Goat's" rooftop terrace, giving us a taste of why, when it comes to food, Chicago is second city to none.

FEAST FAVORITES

Rhubarb-Ginger Soju Sling
CHRIS PANDEL, The Bristol and Balena

Grilled Spring Onion Kimchi with Radishes
STEPHANIE IZARD, Girl & the Goat and Little Goat Diner

Grilled Broccoli Raab and Charred Red Onions
CHRIS PANDEL

Grilled Kalbi Short Ribs
STEPHANIE IZARD

Spicy Pork Dumplings
STEPHANIE IZARD

Rhubarb-Ginger Soju Sling

★ CHRIS PANDEL YIELDS ABOUT ¾ CUP OF GINGER SIMPLE SYRUP, ENOUGH FOR 6 COCKTAILS

FOR THE GINGER SIMPLE SYRUP

½ cup granulated sugar

½ cup peeled and coarsely chopped fresh ginger

FOR EACH COCKTAIL

2 Tbs. rhubarb, finely chopped

3 medium fresh mint leaves plus additional small leaves for garnish

2 oz. soju

You can add more ginger simple syrup to each cocktail if you like. You can also easily double the recipe and keep the syrup in the refrigerator for up to 2 weeks. Soju is a clear, light spirit traditionally distilled from rice, wheat, or barley.

MAKE THE SIMPLE SYRUP

In a medium saucepan, combine the sugar, ginger, and ½ cup water. Bring to a boil over high heat, then reduce to a simmer. Stir until the sugar dissolves. When cool, strain through a fine-mesh sieve into a jar with a lid and refrigerate until ready to use.

MAKE THE COCKTAIL

In a rocks glass, using a muddler or the handle of a wooden spoon, muddle the rhubarb and mint. Add 2 Tbs. of the ginger syrup and enough ice to fill the glass. Add the soju and stir to combine. Serve garnished with the small mint leaves.

Grilled Spring Onion Kimchi with Radishes

★ STEPHANIE IZARD

SERVES 6 AS A SIDE

3 Tbs. gochujang chili paste (Korean spice paste)

3 Tbs. Korean soybean paste (yellow miso)

3 Tbs. mirin

1 clove garlic, grated

½ tsp. finely grated fresh ginger

1½ lb. scallions (about 6 bunches), trimmed and cleaned

3 Tbs. olive oil

4 radishes, thinly sliced (about ⅓ cup)

Kosher salt

"Kimchi," says Chef Izard of the fermented vegetable side dish, "is salty, funky, spicy, and delicious. It sums up what Korean food is all about. Adding kimchi to food that's already grilled provides another layer of flavor."

Heat a gas or charcoal grill to high (500° to 600°F).

In a large bowl, whisk together the chili paste, miso, mirin, garlic, and ginger. Set aside.

Toss the scallions with the oil to coat. Transfer to the grate and grill, covered, turning occasionally, until the scallions are charred and tender, about 4 minutes. Remove from the grill and let cool.

Coarsely chop the scallions and add to the chili paste mixture. Add the radishes and toss until well coated. Season to taste with salt and serve.

Grilled Broccoli Raab and Charred Red Onions

★ CHRIS PANDEL   SERVES 4 AS A SIDE

6 Tbs. olive oil, plus more for the grill

2 cloves garlic, mashed to a paste with the side of a knife

1 large jalapeño, seeded and minced (3 Tbs.)

2 Tbs. fish sauce

Kosher salt

1 medium red onion, trimmed, peeled, and cut crosswise into ½-inch-thick rounds, kept intact

1 lb. broccoli raab, tough bottom stalks trimmed

Lemon wedges, for serving

This is a great way to quickly cook broccoli raab. Its slightly bitter flavor is balanced by the onions and the spicy dressing. If you're a garlic lover, you can leave the garlic in chunks (as Chef Pandel did) instead of mashing it, for a full-on punch of garlic flavor.

In a small bowl, combine 3 Tbs. of the oil, the garlic, jalapeño, and fish sauce. Let the mixture sit for 30 minutes to meld the flavors. Season to taste with salt.

Meanwhile, heat a charcoal or gas grill to medium (350° to 375°F).

Clean and oil the grill. Brush the onion rounds with 1 Tbs. of the oil. Grill the onion, turning occasionally, until charred and slightly softened, about 8 minutes. Transfer to a cutting board, tent with foil, and set aside.

In a large bowl, toss the broccoli raab with the remaining 2 Tbs. oil. Grill the broccoli raab, turning occasionally, about 4 minutes. Transfer to the cutting board with the onion and let rest for about 5 minutes.

Cut the broccoli raab into 4-inch pieces and coarsely chop the onion. Transfer back to the bowl and toss with enough dressing to coat. Arrange on a platter and serve with lemon wedges and the remaining dressing on the side.

Grilled Kalbi Short Ribs

★ STEPHANIE IZARD   SERVES 4 AS A MAIN COURSE, 6 TO 8 AS AN APPETIZER

½ cup malt vinegar

¼ cup sambal oelek

¼ cup olive oil

2 Tbs. fish sauce

2 cloves garlic, mashed to a paste with the side of a knife

3 lb. ½-inch-thick, cross-cut, bone-in short ribs (flanken)

Canola oil

Flaky sea salt, such as Maldon

3 medium scallions, sliced on the diagonal, for garnish

10 small fresh mint leaves, for garnish

If you can't find these flanken-style short ribs, ask your butcher to cut them for you. Chef Izard likes the way fermented malt vinegar complements the fish sauce in this marinade, especially if time is short and you don't have hours to let the beef sit. Even in a few minutes, the marinade adds flavor.

In a large bowl, whisk the malt vinegar, sambal oelek, oil, fish sauce, and garlic. Add the short ribs and toss to coat. Marinate at least 1 hour at room temperature and up to 4 hours in the refrigerator.

Heat a gas or charcoal grill to medium (350° to 375°F). Clean and oil the grate.

Remove the ribs from the marinade, pat dry with paper towels, and lightly brush with oil. Grill the short ribs until just cooked through, about 2 minutes per side. Tent with foil and let rest about 5 minutes.

Cut the ribs between every one or two rib bones. Sprinkle with salt to taste and garnish with the scallions and mint.

"When I was growing up, my mom cooked a lot of fun Asian-inspired things, like moo shu pork. I gravitate back to what my mom did." —Stephanie Izard

Spicy Pork Dumplings

★ STEPHANIE IZARD   SERVES 8 TO 10; YIELDS 30 TO 35 DUMPLINGS

½ cup low-sodium soy sauce

1 tsp. Asian sesame oil

1½ tsp. granulated sugar

1½ tsp. unseasoned rice vinegar

5 medium scallions, thinly sliced on a diagonal (about 1 cup)

½ cup vegetable oil, plus more for frying, as needed

1 lb. ground pork

1 Tbs. finely chopped fresh ginger (from a 1-inch piece)

2 Tbs. fish sauce

2 tsp. finely chopped Thai bird chile (4 to 5 chiles)

2 Tbs. finely chopped fresh mint

2 Tbs. finely chopped fresh cilantro

30 to 35 round dumpling wrappers

Homemade dumplings are easier to make than you think, especially since you can buy the wrappers. When the dumplings are steamed and browned, as these are, they are also called pot stickers.

In a small bowl, combine the soy sauce, sesame oil, sugar, vinegar, and 2 Tbs. of the sliced scallions. Set aside.

Heat 2 Tbs. of the oil in a 12-inch skillet over medium heat. Add the ground pork and cook, stirring occasionally and breaking up the meat with the edge of a spoon, until it is no longer pink, about 5 minutes. Pour off any excess liquid. Add ½ cup of the remaining scallions and the ginger and cook until the scallions begin to soften, about 1 minute. Stir in the fish sauce and the chiles. Remove from the heat and cool completely. Stir in the mint and cilantro.

Keeping the dumpling wrappers covered with a damp kitchen towel, carefully peel 1 wrapper from the stack and put it on a clean work surface. Fill a small bowl with water. Line a large plate with a damp kitchen towel and have another damp towel ready to cover the dumplings.

Drop 2 tsp. of the pork filling in the center of the wrapper. Dip a finger in the water and lightly moisten the edges of the wrapper. Fold it in half and then seal it by pinching along the curved edge. Make a few small pleats on the curved edge of the wrapper by gathering the dough and folding it over onto itself. Seal the pleats by pinching along the top. Put the finished dumpling on the plate and cover with the damp towel. Repeat with the remaining dumpling wrappers and filling.

Position a rack in the center of the oven and heat the oven to 200°F.

Heat 2 Tbs. of the oil in a 12-inch nonstick skillet over medium-high heat until shimmering. Working quickly in batches of about 10, arrange the dumplings belly side down in concentric circles starting from the outer edge. Do not crowd the skillet. Cook until golden brown on the bottom, about 2 minutes. Pour in about ¼ cup water or enough to just cover the

surface of the pan, bring to a boil, cover, and cook until all of the water has been absorbed, 2 to 3 minutes. Remove the lid, reduce the heat to medium, and continue cooking just until the dumplings are puffy and dry and crisp on the bottom, 1 to 2 minutes more.

Loosen the dumplings from the pan with a spatula, transfer to an oven-safe serving platter, and put the platter in the warm oven. Wipe out the skillet and repeat 2 more times with the remaining oil and dumplings.

Sprinkle the dumplings with the remaining scallions and serve with the dipping sauce.

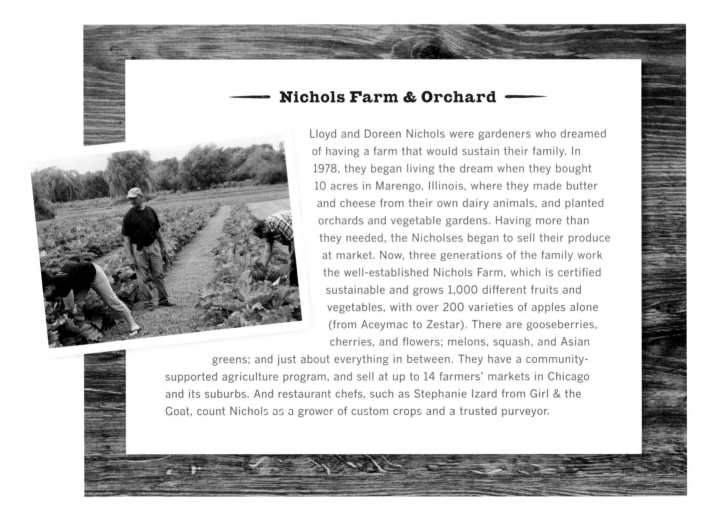

Nichols Farm & Orchard

Lloyd and Doreen Nichols were gardeners who dreamed of having a farm that would sustain their family. In 1978, they began living the dream when they bought 10 acres in Marengo, Illinois, where they made butter and cheese from their own dairy animals, and planted orchards and vegetable gardens. Having more than they needed, the Nicholses began to sell their produce at market. Now, three generations of the family work the well-established Nichols Farm, which is certified sustainable and grows 1,000 different fruits and vegetables, with over 200 varieties of apples alone (from Aceymac to Zestar). There are gooseberries, cherries, and flowers; melons, squash, and Asian greens; and just about everything in between. They have a community-supported agriculture program, and sell at up to 14 farmers' markets in Chicago and its suburbs. And restaurant chefs, such as Stephanie Izard from Girl & the Goat, count Nichols as a grower of custom crops and a trusted purveyor.

— Joong Boo Market —

Whether Chicago cooks need a rice cooker or stockpot; a special ramen, nori, or kimchi; or fresh fruits and vegetables such as Asian greens, pears, and bean sprouts, the meticulously stocked Joong Boo Market, in the Avondale neighborhood, is the place they go. Launched in 1980 as Chicago Food Corp., a wholesaler of Asian foods, the company opened its first retail supermarket as Joong Boo Mart in 1992. Now, in addition to the fresh and frozen seafood and meats, aisle after aisle of fresh and dried noodles, and Korean teas, among thousands of other products, there is a snack bar where you can grab a bowl of *bibimbap* or *dduk gook* (rice cake soup), or a generous helping of *bulgogi* (grilled marinated beef), among more than 20 menu options. There's also a wang mandoo (dumpling) stand.

The accent at Joong Boo is on Korean products, but there are countless other Asian specialties on offer.

"The first time I cooked I felt like I was speaking a language I didn't know I was fluent in." —Gale Gand

BUCHANAN, MI

Chicago chefs Dan Smith and Steve McDonagh, known as the Hearty Boys, know what it takes to combine sophisticated taste with a sense of play. They do it in their catering business, on their Food Network show *The Party Line with the Hearty Boys*, and at SpritzBurger, the restaurant they co-own with pastry chef and Food Network star Gale Gand. When these chefs need to unwind from city life they head 90 miles away, to a lakeside retreat in southern Michigan, an idyllic, unfussy spot where the nineteenth-century mill still grinds corn into cornmeal and the farmers down the way grow tons of heirloom varieties. In other words, they relax by cooking, and at summer's peak we chill along with them, cooking, laughing, and gathering a gang around the picnic table for a true Michigan feast.

FEAST FAVORITES

Cora Sue Collins
STEVE MCDONAGH, SpritzBurger

Stuffed Sirloin Roll with Michigan Cherries and Toasted Hazelnuts
THE HEARTY BOYS

Kale Salad with Pickled Beets, Bacon, Blue Cheese, and Honey-Clove Vinaigrette
THE HEARTY BOYS

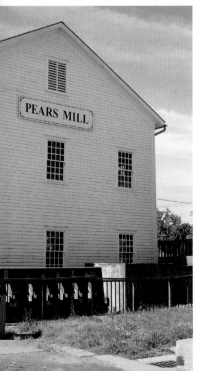

Chive and Cornmeal Spaetzle with Charred Grape Tomatoes and Asparagus
GALE GAND, SpritzBurger

Pavlova with Red-Wine-Roasted Rhubarb and Raspberries
GALE GAND

Cora Sue Collins

★ STEVE MCDONAGH

YIELDS 1 COCKTAIL

4 medium fresh mint leaves, plus 1 small sprig for garnish

½ fl. oz. (1 Tbs.) fresh lemon juice

1 fl. oz. (2 Tbs.) gin

1 fl. oz. (2 Tbs.) elderflower liqueur

4 to 5 fl. oz. (about ½ cup) club soda

Chef McDonagh puts a spin on the classic collins with elderflower liqueur and fresh mint (experiment with the many mint varieties for different flavors). He's named the refreshing cocktail after child actress Cora Sue Collins, who appeared in films alongside the likes of Bette Davis and Greta Garbo in the 1930s and '40s.

In a cocktail shaker, muddle the mint leaves with the lemon juice. Add the gin, elderflower liqueur, and ice to fill the shaker. Shake well.

Fill a collins glass with ice and strain the cocktail shaker into the glass. Top with the club soda and garnish with the mint sprig.

Stuffed Sirloin Roll with Michigan Cherries and Toasted Hazelnuts

★ THE HEARTY BOYS

2 lb. London broil, edges trimmed of excess fat

3 medium cloves garlic, minced

1 tsp. finely grated lemon zest

½ cup plus 2 Tbs. extra-virgin olive oil

3 sprigs thyme

1 sprig rosemary

1 sprig sage

4 oz. shiitake mushrooms, stemmed and coarsely chopped

12 oz. Swiss chard or kale, stemmed and coarsely chopped

Kosher salt and freshly ground black pepper

2 medium shallots, thinly sliced

¾ cup dried cherries

½ cup red wine

2 oz. (4 Tbs.) unsalted butter

½ cup toasted hazelnuts, coarsely chopped

As an alternative stuffing to Swiss chard or kale, you can use very fresh beet greens or ramp leaves, as Chef Smith does. He likes the way the savory stuffed sirloin gets a subtle sweet touch with the cherry and red-wine sauce, and a lively crunch with hazelnuts.

Place the meat on your cutting board and arrange it so that the grains run up and down. Position your knife halfway up the side and begin cutting through the meat until you get 1 inch from the edge. Open the meat like a book and press down on the center to flatten.

Cover the top of the meat with plastic wrap and pound it with a meat mallet to a ⅜-inch thickness, being careful not to tear the meat. Remove the plastic wrap and dock both sides of the meat with a fork all over.

In a large baking dish or a large reusable zip-top bag, add the garlic, lemon zest, and ½ cup of the oil. Break the thyme, rosemary, and sage sprigs by hand, crushing the leaves to release the oils, and place them in the marinade. Add the meat to the baking dish or bag and turn in the marinade to coat both sides. Refrigerate for 8 to 16 hours.

Heat 1 Tbs. of the oil in a 12-inch skillet over medium heat. Add the mushrooms and cook until softened, about 3 minutes. Add the chard, tossing, and cook until wilted, about 3 minutes. Season to taste with salt and pepper and set aside until cool to the touch.

Prepare a grill for indirect cooking over high heat (500° to 600°F). Turn off one of the burners to create a cool zone.

Remove the meat from the marinade and place it on a cutting board. Remove any of the herb sprigs that have adhered to the meat and season both sides with salt and pepper. Spread the cooled chard mixture in a thin even layer over the cut surface of the meat. Working with the grain, roll the meat up tightly, like a jellyroll. Tie the roulade with butcher's twine in 1- to 2-inch intervals.

Place the roulade on the hot side of the grill and cook for about 4 minutes per side on 4 sides. Move to the cooler side of the grill and

continue to cook until an internal thermometer reads 145°F, about 20 minutes. Transfer to a cutting board and tent with foil; let rest for 10 to 15 minutes before slicing.

Meanwhile, heat the remaining 1 Tbs. of oil in a 10-inch skillet over medium heat. Add the shallot and cook until softened, about 2 minutes. Add the cherries and the red wine and simmer until reduced by half, 4 to 6 minutes. Remove from the heat, and whisk in the butter, until completely incorporated. Season to taste with salt and pepper.

Cut the butcher's twine from the meat and slice the roll into ½-inch-thick pieces. Arrange the meat on a large serving platter and spoon the cherry sauce over the top. Garnish with the hazelnuts and serve.

—— Blue Star Produce ——

Chefs Gand, McDonagh, and Smith love Buchanan's Blue Star Produce, where Mark and Jennifer Collins grow more than 100 varieties of heirloom vegetables and fruit on their 40 acres—such as Detroit Dark Red beets and Suyo Long cukes, Freckles lettuce and Charentais melons, Purple Beauty peppers and more than 20 varieties of tomatoes.

Mark grew up on the farm, where his family grew peaches and wine grapes using traditional methods. But after Mark studied agriculture at Andrews University, and he and his wife took over the land, in 2007, the couple decided to concentrate on heirloom varieties and make what they grew Certified Naturally Grown produce, meaning they don't use any synthetic herbicides, pesticides, fertilizers, antibiotics, hormones, or genetically modified organisms.

Blue Star has two CSAs, one of which is devoted exclusively to tomatoes. They donate their excess produce to community organizations and share their seeds and plants with community gardeners.

Kale Salad with Pickled Beets, Bacon, Blue Cheese, and Honey-Clove Vinaigrette

★ THE HEARTY BOYS   SERVES 8 TO 10

Massaging the dressed kale with your hands helps to break down the tough nature of the greens, leaving them more smooth and less bitter.

FOR THE PICKLED BEETS

1½ cups cider vinegar

¾ cup granulated sugar

1 Tbs. fennel seeds

1 Tbs. caraway seeds

1 Tbs. black peppercorns

1½ tsp. yellow mustard seeds

5 bay leaves

1 cinnamon stick

Kosher salt

1 lb. baby beets (about 1 inch diameter), peeled and very thinly sliced on a mandoline

FOR THE DRESSING

¼ cup cider vinegar

1 Tbs. honey

¼ tsp. ground cloves

¾ cup extra-virgin olive oil

Kosher salt and freshly ground black pepper

FOR THE SALAD

1 lb. lacinato kale, washed, stemmed, and torn into bite-size pieces

1 lb. slab bacon, cut lengthwise into ½-inch slices and crosswise into ½-inch-thick lardons

4 oz. blue cheese, crumbled into large pieces

Kosher salt and freshly ground black pepper

PICKLE THE BEETS

In a 3-quart saucepan, combine the vinegar, sugar, fennel and caraway seeds, peppercorns, mustard seeds, bay leaves, cinnamon, 2 Tbs. salt, and ½ cup water. Bring to a boil, stirring to dissolve the sugar. Reduce the heat to a simmer and cook for 5 minutes. Place the beets in a medium bowl and pour the pickling liquid through a sieve over the beets, discarding the solids. Let sit at room temperature for at least one hour or up to 1 week, covered, in the refrigerator.

MAKE THE DRESSING

In a medium bowl, whisk together the vinegar, honey, and cloves. While whisking, slowly drizzle in the oil until emulsified. Season generously with salt and pepper.

ASSEMBLE THE SALAD

Put the kale in a large serving bowl and toss with ¼ cup of the dressing to lightly coat. Using your hands, lightly massage the dressing into the leaves. Let the kale sit to soften for 30 to 60 minutes.

Meanwhile, put half the bacon in a single layer in a 12-inch skillet over medium heat. Cook, turning occasionally, until the lardons are crisp, about 5 minutes. Transfer to a plate lined with paper towels to drain. Repeat with the remaining bacon.

Put the cheese, pickled beets, and lardons in the bowl with the kale. Add enough of the remaining dressing to coat evenly and toss well. Season to taste with salt and pepper, transfer to a platter, and serve.

Chive and Cornmeal Spaetzle with Charred Grape Tomatoes and Asparagus

★ GALE GAND   SERVES 8

Kosher salt and freshly ground black pepper

¼ cup extra-virgin olive oil

1½ lb. asparagus, trimmed and sliced on a bias into 1½-inch pieces

2 pints grape tomatoes

3 large eggs

¾ cup whole milk

2 Tbs. Dijon mustard

8 oz. (1¾ cups) all-purpose flour

¼ cup cornmeal

¼ tsp. nutmeg

1 tsp. finely chopped chives, plus more for garnish

3 Tbs. fresh-squeezed lemon juice

2 medium cloves garlic, mashed to a paste with the side of a knife

Chef Gand adds cornmeal to her spaetzle (a traditional German dumpling) to give it added texture and a bit of crunch. With the tomatoes, she sautés them until, she says, they "jump in the pan."

Bring a large pot of well-salted water to a boil.

Meanwhile, heat 1 Tbs. of the oil in a 12-inch skillet over medium heat. Add the asparagus, season with salt and pepper, and cook, tossing occasionally, until tender, about 5 minutes. Transfer to a large serving bowl. Increase the heat to medium high and swirl in 1 Tbs. of oil. Add the tomatoes, season with salt and pepper, and cook until the tomatoes are blistered and beginning to split, about 6 minutes. Add the tomatoes to the bowl with the asparagus and set aside.

Whisk together the eggs, milk, and mustard in a large bowl. Add the flour, cornmeal, nutmeg, chives, and 1 tsp. salt and whisk until completely combined. Place a spaetzle maker over the boiling water. Push the dough through the holes, letting it fall into the water below. (If you don't have a spaetzle maker, use a rubber spatula to push the dough through the holes of a colander set over the pot of water.) The dough will form small dumplings as it drops into the water. Allow the spaetzle to rise to the surface and float for about 3 minutes. Remove the spaetzle from the boiling water with a spider or slotted spoon to the bowl with the vegetables and toss well.

In a small bowl whisk together the lemon juice, the remaining 2 Tbs. oil, the garlic, ½ tsp. salt, and ¼ tsp. pepper. Add to the spaetzle and toss well to combine. Season to taste with salt and pepper and sprinkle with the additional chives.

Pavlova with Red-Wine-Roasted Rhubarb and Raspberries

★ GALE GAND

SERVES 8 TO 10

FOR THE PAVLOVA SHELL

4 large egg whites, at room temperature

⅛ tsp. cream of tartar

1 cup granulated sugar

1½ tsp. cornstarch

Finely ground sea salt

½ tsp. pure vanilla extract

1 Tbs. raspberry vinegar

FOR THE ROASTED RHUBARB AND RASPBERRY TOPPING

¼ cup light-bodied red wine

¼ cup granulated sugar

½ vanilla bean, split

1 tsp. cornstarch

¼ tsp. ground cinnamon

Kosher salt

11 oz. rhubarb (about 3 large stalks), washed, trimmed, and cut into 1-inch pieces

Three 6-oz. containers fresh raspberries (about 3 cups)

FOR THE WHIPPED CREAM

1¼ cups heavy cream

2 Tbs. confectioners' sugar

Edible flowers, for garnish (optional)

Crisp on the outside and chewy on the inside, the pavlova shell is a classic frothy meringue. You can make it ahead and store it, completely cooled, in an airtight container for up to 3 days. When it comes to pricey vanilla beans, Chef Gand reuses them in other recipes—she simply rinses them and pats them dry.

MAKE THE PAVLOVA SHELL

Position a rack in the center of the oven and heat the oven to 250°F.

Line a baking sheet with parchment. Draw an 8-inch circle in the center of the parchment and then turn the paper over (you'll still see the circle).

In a stand mixer fitted with the whisk attachment, beat the egg whites and cream of tartar on high speed until foamy, about 1 minute. Sift together the sugar, cornstarch, and a pinch of salt. With the mixer running, gradually add the dry ingredients 1 Tbs. at a time to the egg whites until completely incorporated. Add the vanilla extract and vinegar and continue beating on high speed until stiff, smooth, glossy peaks form, scraping down the bowl occasionally, about 8 minutes more. Test to see if the sugar is fully dissolved by rubbing a bit of the meringue between your thumb and index finger. The mixture should feel smooth and grit free.

Spoon the meringue into the center of the parchment circle and spread to fill the circle. Use the back of the spoon or a small offset spatula to smooth the top and sides of the meringue, making the center slightly concave.

Transfer the meringue to the oven and bake until it has puffed slightly and the surface is lightly browned and dry, rotating halfway through baking, about 1½ hours. Turn the oven off and let the pavlova cool in the oven to room temperature, at least 45 minutes, or up to overnight.

MERINGUE MUSTS

Don't bother making meringue on a rainy day. A meringue is hygroscopic, meaning it absorbs moisture from the environment. On a humid day, meringue toppings will be more likely to weep, and baked meringues may be sticky instead of crisp.

Keep any yolk out of the whites. The fat in the yolks interferes with the bonding of the protein molecules in the whites, making the foam less light and stable. Separate each egg over a small bowl to be sure the white is free of egg yolk before combining with other whites. The yolks are less likely to break and contaminate the whites if you separate them while they're cold.

MAKE THE ROASTED RHUBARB AND RASPBERRY TOPPING

Position a rack in the center of the oven and heat the oven to 400°F. In an 8 x 8-inch baking dish, combine the wine, sugar, vanilla bean, corn-starch, cinnamon, and a pinch of salt until dissolved. Add the rhubarb, toss to coat, and roast until tender, about 25 minutes. Remove from the oven and let cool completely. Discard the vanilla bean. Add the rasp-berries to the roasted rhubarb and gently fold with a spatula to combine.

MAKE THE WHIPPED CREAM

In a medium chilled bowl, whisk together the heavy cream and the sugar until medium-stiff peaks form.

To serve, place the meringue on a cake stand. Spoon the whipped cream onto the center of the meringue. Top with the rhubarb-raspberry mixture and garnish with the edible flowers, if using.

California is the land of plenty, and chefs and home cooks across the country reap the benefits of its perfect growing conditions. And when you're a cook who just happens to live there . . . well, the possibilities seem endless. Luscious stone fruit grows in the Central Valley, and vineyards flourish in Napa and Sonoma counties. Chiles and avocados and lemons are there for the picking. And Pacific Coast fishermen keep the wild-caught salmon coming. The rich mix of ethnicities here also means that there is a wealth of Asian and Southeast Asian foods, of Latin and Mideastern flavors, and so much more. In our California feasts we traveled from north to south, dipping into the markets, groves, and farms along the way with chefs whose range truly represents the diversity of this state. We explore Mexican cuisine with *Too Hot Tamales*', Mary Sue Milliken and Susan Feniger; Cuban with Anthony Lamas; Thai with Jeffrey Saad; and what can only be considered the finest of New American cooking with the likes of Duskie Estes, Brooke Williamson, and many others. Their recipes will definitely get you in a California state of mind.

"Start with
deliciousness
and layer it up!"

—Ravi Kapur

SECRET SEA COVE, BAY AREA, CA

A stunning San Francisco Bay area sea cove is the setting for this feast led by Ravi Kapur, chef-owner of San Francisco's Liholiho Yacht Club, and former star of the city's pop-up restaurant scene. Kapur made great sense as a guest chef for this meal, an event with Outstanding in the Field, a "restaurant without walls" that brings the dinner table to the source—farms, gardens, mountaintops, islands, ranches, and even sea caves. A world of challenges comes with cooking at the beach, but the Hawaii-born Kapur brings a sense of adventure and fun to every meal he makes. As guests literally soak up the atmosphere, with the Pacific lapping at their feet, the prettiest potato chip you've ever seen is passed as an hors d'oeuvre, and locally sourced seafood (what else at a seaside dinner?) gets a delicate Asian treatment to keep the meal serenely spectacular.

FEAST FAVORITES

Fresh Ricotta with Peas and Tarragon on Potato Crisps

Halibut and Avocado Tartare on Nori Chips

Rare Grilled Salmon Fillets with Asian Slaw

Fresh Ricotta with Peas and Tarragon on Potato Crisps

YIELDS 40 TO 50 HORS D'OEUVRES

FOR THE TOPPING

2 cups fresh or frozen (10 oz.) shelled peas

1 cup fresh whole-milk ricotta cheese

½ oz. Parmigiano-Reggiano, finely grated (½ cup using a rasp grater)

1 Tbs. chopped fresh tarragon leaves

Kosher salt and freshly ground black pepper

2 oz. microgreens (about 2 cups), for garnish

White truffle oil for drizzling (optional)

FOR THE POTATO CRISPS

40–50 sturdy store-bought potato chips, such as Terra® brand

The lightness of fresh peas and ricotta makes this gently herbed appetizer satisfying but not filling and turns the notion of heavy chips and dip on its head.

MAKE THE TOPPING

Have a bowl of ice water ready. Bring a 2-quart saucepan of water to a boil, add the peas, and cook until just tender, about 5 minutes. Drain the peas and transfer to the bowl of ice water to stop the cooking. Drain well.

Put the peas in a medium bowl and coarsely mash with a fork. Add the ricotta, Parmigiano, tarragon, 1½ tsp. salt and 1 tsp. pepper and stir to combine. The topping can be made 1 day ahead and kept in the refrigerator, covered.

TO SERVE

Dollop a heaping teaspoon of the topping on each chip, top with a pinch of microgreens and a drop of truffle oil, if using. Serve immediately.

Halibut and Avocado Tartare on Nori Chips

★ RAVI KAPUR

YIELDS ABOUT 30 HORS D'OEUVRES

2 cups vegetable oil

1 Tbs. cornstarch

6 full sheets of toasted nori (dried seaweed), approximately 7½ x 8¼ inches

Kosher salt

½ lb. fresh skinless halibut fillet, cut into ⅓-inch dice

1 Tbs. Asian sesame oil

½ Tbs. tamari (wheat-free soy sauce) or soy sauce

1 ripe avocado cut into ⅓-inch dice

Toasted white or black sesame seeds for sprinkling

Nori breaks out of the traditional sushi role in a crisp fried version that blends its unique sea flavors with the ultra-fresh halibut and smooth avocado.

Put the vegetable oil in a 2- to 3-quart saucepan and heat the oil over medium-high heat until a deep-fat/candy thermometer clipped to the side of the saucepan registers 350°F. Line a baking sheet with paper towels.

Mix the cornstarch with 2 Tbs. of cold water until it is dissolved. Lightly brush one long half of a nori sheet with the cornstarch-water mixture. Fold it in half lengthwise, pressing so the two sides adhere. Position the nori sheet so that one long edge is facing you. Using a ruler and a small paring knife, mark the bottom long edge of the nori at 2½-inch intervals. Working from left to right, mark the top edge of the nori once at 1¼-inch, and then at the subsequent 2½-inch intervals. These marks will fall halfway between the bottom edge marks. Using a large knife, make diagonal cuts from the bottom to the top and then top to bottom across the length of the nori to make five 2½-inch triangles (discard the half triangles at the ends). Repeat with the remaining nori sheets.

Fry 2 to 3 nori triangles at a time in the hot oil until they become crisp, about 20 seconds (they will shrink slightly). Drain on paper towels and sprinkle with salt.

Gently stir the halibut with the sesame oil, tamari, and ½ tsp. salt in a medium bowl. Fold in the avocado. Adjust the seasoning, if necessary.

Dollop 1 Tbs. of the fish mixture on each nori triangle and garnish with sesame seeds. Serve immediately.

Rare Grilled Salmon Fillets with Asian Slaw

★ RAVI KAPUR

SERVES 4

FOR THE SLAW

2 cups canola oil, plus more for the grill

7 fresh square wonton wrappers, cut into ⅛-inch strips

¼ cup fresh lime juice (2 medium limes)

1 Tbs. granulated sugar

1 Tbs. fish sauce

Kosher salt

½ white cabbage, halved lengthwise, cored and very thinly sliced (about 8 cups)

1 large carrot, peeled and coarsely shredded (about 1 cup)

½ cup packed fresh Thai basil leaves, thinly sliced

½ cup peanuts, preferably raw, coarsely chopped

1 to 2 medium jalapeño chiles, coarsely chopped, including seeds

1 fresh red Fresno pepper, seeded, ribs removed, and coarsely chopped

FOR THE SALMON

Four 6-oz. skin-on salmon fillets

Kosher salt and freshly ground black pepper

2 Tbs. olive oil

1 Tbs. all-purpose flour

Shredded cabbage, Thai basil, peanuts, jalapeño chiles, and a Fresno pepper create a slaw that's perfectly crunchy and bright with a bit of heat—just what a mellow-tasting salmon calls for.

MAKE THE SLAW

Heat the canola oil in a 3-quart pot over medium-high heat until a strip of wonton dropped into the oil bubbles vigorously. Add the wontons in 3 small batches, stirring gently, until golden, 20 to 30 seconds, and transfer with a slotted spoon to paper towels to drain. Set aside.

In a large bowl, whisk the lime juice, sugar, fish sauce, and 1 tsp. salt until the sugar and salt are dissolved. Add the remaining ingredients except for the wonton strips and toss to coat. Let sit to soften slightly, about 30 minutes.

COOK THE SALMON

Prepare a charcoal or gas grill fire for direct grilling over medium-high heat (about 400°F), or heat a grill pan on top of the stove. Oil the grill grate well.

Pat the salmon dry and season with salt and pepper. Spread the olive oil in a small, rimmed baking sheet and spread the flour on a plate. Dip the fillets, skin side down, in the flour, knocking off any excess; then put on the oiled sheet, turning once to coat both sides. Leave on sheet.

Grill the salmon, skin side down. For rare only, loosely cover with foil, until the sides are opaque but the top is still translucent, 7 to 8 minutes. For fully cooked salmon, turn the fillets over and cook for an additional 2 to 3 minutes.

Garnish the slaw with the fried wonton strips and serve with the salmon.

── Outstanding in the Field ──

Turning the farm-to-table movement into a table-to-farm movement, Outstanding in the Field is a series of events that brings people who love good food to farmers who produce it and chefs who know how to cook it. At tables that seem to stretch for a mile across a field or a meadow or a beach at sunset, like our Moveable Feast, bread is broken and connections are made.

Jim Denevan, whose brother Bill is an organic grower, did his first Outstanding dinner in a Santa Cruz, California, farm field back in 1999. By 2003, the event was going coast-to-coast (with a crew traveling around in a vintage red-and-white bus), partnering with guest chefs like Frank Stitt (of Birmingham, Alabama's, Highlands Bar and Grill), Gabrielle Hamilton (of New York City's Prune), and San Francisco's Ravi Kapur, doing 90 plus table-to-farm dinners a year.

> *"We don't know how to shop in Sonoma. We harvest, forage, or gather."*
> —Duskie Estes

HEALDSBURG, CA

You might say that chefs Duskie Estes, of Zazu, and Mark Stark, of Willi's Wine Bar (and several other Sonoma restaurants), have got game. And they always seem to be at the top of it, whether they're kicking off the day of the feast with a game of bocci, gathering goat's-milk cheese from the source, shaping pillowy gnocchi, or braising duck in a richer than rich barbecue sauce. The best part is, they make it all look like play. Sonoma being one of the country's top playgrounds for those who love great wine and great food, Estes and Stark are right at home, which the outdoor feast they throw at Davis Family Vineyards demonstrates deliciously.

FEAST FAVORITES

Watermelon and Goat Cheese Salad
PETE EVANS, HOST

Coffee Barbecue Duck and Smoked Cheddar Polenta
MARK STARK, Stark Restaurants

Goat Cheese Gnocchi and Zasugo (Pork & Short Rib Braise)
DUSKIE ESTES, Zazu Restaurant + Farm

Watermelon and Goat Cheese Salad

★ PETE EVANS   SERVES 4

5 lb. watermelon

¼ cup plus 2 Tbs. Banyuls or
   red-wine vinegar

2 Tbs. pine nuts

1 finger radish

1 Tbs. minced shallots

½ Tbs. Dijon mustard

½ tsp. honey

3½ Tbs. extra-virgin olive oil

1 Tbs. white truffle oil

1 cup loosely packed
   watercress

1 cup loosely packed arugula

1 cup loosely packed
   microgreens

1½ oz. goat cheese, crumbled

Peppery greens complement the sweet, clean flavor of watermelon in this salad topped with creamy goat cheese.

Cut the watermelon into 1-inch chunks and set aside.

Boil ¼ cup of the vinegar in a small saucepan over medium heat until sticky, add the pine nuts and mix with a spoon to coat. Spread the mixture onto a small baking sheet, and separate the nuts. Let cool completely.

Thinly slice the radish and place in a small bowl of ice water.

Combine the remaining 2 Tbs. vinegar, the shallot, Dijon, honey, and both of the oils in a small bowl and whisk until emulsified. Combine the watercress, arugula, and microgreens in a medium bowl, and gently toss with just enough of the dressing to coat.

Arrange the watermelon chunks on a platter. Crumble the goat cheese over the watermelon. Drain the radish. Arrange the greens and radish over the watermelon and then sprinkle with the pine nuts. Drizzle with the remaining dressing and serve.

Coffee Barbecue Duck and Smoked Cheddar Polenta

★ MARK STARK SERVES 4

FOR THE COFFEE BARBECUE SAUCE

1 Tbs. unsalted butter

1 small onion, halved and sliced

3 medium cloves garlic, chopped

1 cup ketchup

½ cup Worcestershire sauce

½ cup strong brewed coffee

½ cup apple-cider vinegar

½ cup dark brown sugar

1½ tsp. chili powder

¼ tsp. kosher salt

FOR THE DUCK

Four 14-oz. Muscovy duck legs (available at dartagnan.com)

Kosher salt and freshly ground black pepper

1 Tbs. olive oil

1 large yellow onion, halved and sliced

6 medium cloves garlic, smashed and peeled

2 cups chicken broth

2 cups Coffee Barbecue Sauce

½ cup chopped cilantro, plus 2 Tbs. leaves for garnish

1 Tbs. cold unsalted butter

Smoked Cheddar Polenta (p. 158)

There isn't a pronounced coffee flavor in this barbecue sauce; it simply adds depth. Serve the duck, as Chef Stark does, over smoky polenta (recipe on p. 158). Make sure to save your leftover duck fat (stored either in the refrigerator or freezer)—it's great for frying potatoes in.

MAKE THE SAUCE

Melt the butter in a 2½- to 3-quart saucepan over medium heat until the foam subsides. Add the onion and garlic and cook, stirring, until golden, 6 to 8 minutes. Add the remaining ingredients, bring to a simmer, and continue to simmer, uncovered, stirring and scraping down the sides of the pan occasionally, 45 minutes. Cool, then purée in a blender until smooth.

The barbecue sauce will keep, in a tightly sealed jar or container, in the refrigerator for several weeks.

MAKE THE DUCK

Arrange a rack in the center of the oven and heat the oven to 350°F.

Pat the duck dry and season it all over with 1 tsp. salt and ½ tsp. pepper, total.

Heat the oil in an oven-safe 12-inch skillet (2 inches deep) or braisier over medium heat until shimmering hot. Working in batches, if necessary, put the duck legs, skin side down, in the pan and cook, turning once, until the skin is a deep golden brown and the fat is rendered, about 10 minutes. Transfer, skin side up, to a plate.

Drain all but 2 Tbs. fat from the pan (keep the excess for another use). Add the onion and garlic to the pan and cook, stirring, over medium heat until golden, 6 to 8 minutes. Add the chicken broth, barbecue sauce, and chopped cilantro and bring to a simmer. Return the duck legs, skin side up, to the pan, nestling them in the sauce. Cover the pan tightly with a fitted lid or foil, put in the oven, and braise until the meat is tender, about 1½ hours.

Remove the lid and let the duck cool in the braising liquid, about 1 hour. When cool enough to handle, shred the meat, discarding the

skin and bones. Strain the sauce through a sieve into a degreasing cup, pressing on and then discarding the solids. In a 2- to 3-quart saucepan, combine the meat and just enough of the defatted sauce to coat the duck well (about 2 cups; reserve the remainder for another use) and reheat. Swirl in the butter until incorporated and transfer to a serving dish. Garnish with the cilantro leaves and serve.

smoked cheddar polenta

SERVES 4

1 large ear corn, shucked and snapped in half

1 cup whole milk, plus more as needed

1 cup water

½ cup polenta (not quick cooking)

1 oz. extra-sharp white cheddar, coarsely grated (¼ cup)

1 oz. smoked cheddar, coarsely grated (¼ cup)

1 Tbs. unsalted butter

Kosher salt and freshly ground black pepper

Chicken broth, as needed (optional)

Fresh corn adds texture to this classic ground-corn dish. Polenta leftovers make a great second-day meal—use them as a bed for sautéed vegetables.

Position an oven rack in the center of the oven, and heat the oven to 350°F.

Using the coarse holes of a box grater, grate the corn directly into an oven-safe, 2- to 3-quart, heavy-duty saucepan. Add the milk and water and bring to a simmer over medium heat. Slowly sprinkle in the polenta, whisking constantly (do not add quickly and all at once or it will become lumpy), until the mixture just begins to thicken, about 2 minutes. Cover pan tightly with a double layer of foil or a tight fitting lid, place in the oven, and bake for 45 minutes.

Remove the pan from the oven and whisk in the cheeses and butter. Season to taste with salt and pepper. The polenta should have the consistency of soft mashed potatoes. If not, adjust with more milk or chicken broth. Keep warm until ready to serve.

SALTY SPICE RUB

At his restaurant, Chef Stark uses a "red salt" spice rub for duck: a mixture of kosher salt, smoked paprika, sweet paprika, and a touch of cayenne pepper.

— Davis Family Vineyards —

Wine critic Robert Parker called the Davis Family Vineyards' Soul Patch Pinot Noir "an intense, rich, and flat-out beautiful wine." The *Chicago Sun-Times* critic W. Peter Hoyne declared it "among the five most memorable Pinots that I have ever tasted." It seems the Davis family knows a thing or two about producing great Pinot Noir (as well as old-vine Zinfandel and a Marsanne/Roussane/Viognier blend, among others).

When Guy Davis and his wife, Judy, launched their Russian River Valley winery, in 1995, they brought a shared love for great wines, more than a decade of tasting and marketing wine, and a working relationship with artisan winemakers.

Son Cole Davis is the vineyard's cellarmaster, and son Cooper, while studying at Sonoma State University's Wine Business Institute, helps run the tasting room and the farm. He also cooks part-time alongside chefs Duskie Estes and John Stewart at their seasonal outpost of restaurant Zazu at the vineyard.

"Wine is an essential element in a rich and passionate life," says Guy Davis, who, along with his family, puts that philosophy into practice daily.

Goat Cheese Gnocchi and Zasugo (Pork & Short Rib Braise)

★ DUSKIE ESTES   SERVES 8 TO 10

FOR THE ZASUGO

5 lb. meaty bone-in beef short
   ribs

3 lb. bone-in pork shoulder

Kosher salt and freshly ground
   black pepper

¼ cup olive oil

2 medium onions, chopped
   (about 2 cups)

2 medium carrots, chopped
   (about 1 cup)

3 medium stalks celery,
   chopped (about 1 cup)

6 medium cloves garlic,
   coarsely chopped (about
   2 Tbs.)

1 cup dry red wine

Two 14-oz. cans diced
   tomatoes (28 oz. total)

1½ cups lower-sodium chicken
   broth

2 tsp. chile oil, preferably
   Calabrian (optional)

2 bay leaves

1 tsp. chopped fresh oregano

½ tsp. crushed red pepper
   flakes

12 oz. (1½ cups) unsalted
   butter, cut into pieces

FOR THE GNOCCHI

1 lb. fresh goat cheese,
   crumbled

2 large eggs, lightly beaten

Kosher salt and freshly ground
   pepper   →

Sugo is a long-simmered Italian sauce that often includes meats, such as pork or beef. Chef Estes's delicious version is aptly called zasugo, after her Sonoma County-based restaurant Zazu. This rich, tender meat sauce ladled over feathery-light goat cheese gnocchi will satisfy your innermost desires for warmth and comfort.

MAKE THE ZASAGU

Position a rack in the center of the oven, and heat the oven to 350°F.

Season the meat generously with salt and pepper. Heat the olive oil in a 7-quart Dutch oven or heavy-duty pot over medium-high heat until it's shimmering hot. Sear the pork shoulder on all sides until browned and caramelized, about 6 minutes. Remove the meat to a large plate. Sear the beef short ribs, in batches if necessary, on all sides until browned and caramelized, about 5 minutes per batch. Transfer the ribs to the plate.

Reduce the heat to medium. Add the onion, carrot, and celery to the pot and cook, stirring often, until softened, 4 to 5 minutes. Add the garlic and cook, stirring often, until fragrant, 1 to 2 minutes. Add the wine, stirring to scrape up any browned bits, and cook until reduced by half. Return the meat to the pot, add the tomatoes, chicken broth, chile oil, bay leaves, oregano, and red pepper flakes. Cover and bake until the meat is very tender and pulls away from the bone easily, 3 to 3½ hours.

MAKE THE GNOCCHI

Combine the goat cheese, eggs, and a pinch of salt and pepper in a medium bowl. Using an electric mixer, beat on medium speed until blended, scraping down sides of the bowl as necessary. Add the flour, 2 to 3 tablespoons at a time, beating on low speed between additions, until it is absorbed and a soft, pliable dough begins to form. You may not need all the flour. The dough should be moist and slightly sticky.

Turn the dough out onto a lightly floured work surface and form it into a ball. Cut the ball into quarters. Cover three of the dough pieces in plastic wrap and refrigerate. Roll the remaining piece of dough into a

1½ cups all-purpose flour, more for the work surface and baking sheet

Extra-virgin olive oil, for the cooked gnocchi

FOR SERVING

7 oz. (7 packed cups) baby arugula

2 Tbs. extra-virgin olive oil

Kosher salt and freshly ground black pepper

1 oz. Parmigiano-Reggiano, finely grated (½ cup on a rasp grater)

MAKE AHEAD

You can make the gnocchi and the zasugo up to a day ahead. Refrigerate the zasugo (before adding the butter) once cool. Reheat and add the butter before serving. Arrange the gnocchi on a lightly floured baking sheet, cover with plastic wrap, and refrigerate. You can also freeze the gnocchi for up to several months: freeze on the baking sheet until firm, about 1 hour, and then transfer the frozen gnocchi to an airtight plastic bag and return to the freezer.

1-inch-thick rope, 20 to 24 inches long, dusting with flour as needed. Using a sharp knife, cut the rope into ¾-inch pieces and transfer them to a lightly floured baking sheet. Repeat this process with the remaining dough pieces. If desired, roll each piece over a gnocchi paddle to make ridges. Lightly dust the gnocchi with flour and let rest at room temperature for about 10 minutes.

SHRED THE ZASAGU

Remove the pot from the oven. Transfer the meat to a large bowl, and, using tongs, pull off and discard the skin, fat, cartilage, and bones. Separate the meat into medium-size chunks with the tongs.

Skim the fat from the top of the liquid in the pot and return the meat to the pot. Add the butter and swirl the pot until the butter is melted and blended with the braising liquid. Adjust the seasoning if necessary, cover, and keep warm over low heat.

COOK THE GNOCCHI

Bring a 6- to 8-quart pot of well-salted water to a boil.

Set aside a large bowl for the gnocchi. Drop as many gnocchi into the boiling water as will fit without crowding. When the gnocchi rise to the top, continue cooking until tender, for another 1 to 1½ minutes. With a slotted spoon, transfer the gnocchi to the reserved bowl. Drizzle with a little olive oil and gently stir with a rubber spatula to coat. Repeat this procedure with the remaining gnocchi.

TO SERVE

Using tongs, transfer the meat to a deep serving dish. Spoon some of the braising liquid over the gnocchi and toss to coat. Spoon the gnocchi over the meat, and pour the remaining braising liquid over the top.

Toss the arugula with the olive oil in a large bowl, and season with salt and pepper to taste.

Arrange the arugula on top of the meat and gnocchi and garnish with the cheese.

— Redwood Hill Farm —

With its mixed herd of goats—Alpine, LaManca, Nubian, and Saanen—Redwood Hill Farm makes award-winning artisan cheeses (from fresh chèvre to a buttery bucheret), yogurt, and kefir. The Bice family has been breaking ground with their sustainable dairy farm for 45 years. In the 1960s and early '70s, Redwood was ahead of the curve with its bottled goat's milk and its kefir (the first goat's-milk kefir in the country). Daughter Jennifer Bice (who had raised goats since she was a child) and her partner Steven Schack took over the farm and in 1982 introduced the nation's first goat's-milk yogurt. In 2003, Redwood qualified as the first goat dairy to use the Certified Humane Raised and Handled label. Jennifer Bice was inducted into the American Cheese Society Academy of Cheese as a pioneer of artisan goat cheese in the U.S.

"I can't think of anything better than lying under an avocado tree eating avocados and drinking Syrah!" —Susan Feniger

TEMECULA, CA

Wherever the *Too Hot Tamales* chefs Susan Feniger and Mary Sue Milliken cook, it's bound to be a good time. The Border Grill chefs have been cooking together since 1981, and their sense of teamwork, know-how about authentic Mexican cuisine, and playfulness make a day spent with them a feast in every way. The scene is Rancho Bella Santé, in the southern mountains of Temecula, where avocados and lemons are at the chefs' fingertips. But before we fire up the grill back at the ranch, we hit the Santa Monica Farmers' Market, one of the country's best, to snatch up artichokes and collards, mint and tomatoes, laughing and learning all the way.

FEAST FAVORITES

Lamb Sausage Patties with Avocado Relish
PETE EVANS, HOST

Heirloom Bean Tostadas with Crispy Avocado
SUSAN FENIGER AND MARY SUE MILLIKEN, Border Grill

Grilled Salmon Wrapped in Collards with Tomato-Mint Salsa and Tzatziki
SUSAN FENIGER AND MARY SUE MILLIKEN

Lemon Soufflé with Rhubarb-Vanilla Compote
SUSAN FENIGER AND MARY SUE MILLIKEN

Lamb Sausage Patties with Avocado Relish

★ PETE EVANS   SERVES 6 TO 12 AS AN APPETIZER; YIELDS 12 PATTIES AND 2 CUPS RELISH

FOR THE AVOCADO RELISH

2 firm, ripe Hass avocados, peeled, seeded, and cut into ½-inch dice

⅓ cup seeded and finely chopped red bell pepper

¼ cup finely chopped red onion

2 Tbs. coarsely chopped fresh cilantro

1 large lemon, grated to yield 1 Tbs. zest and squeezed to yield 3 Tbs. juice

2 tsp. seeded and finely chopped jalepeño

2 tsp. seeded and finely chopped Fresno chile

1 tsp. seeded and finely chopped serrano chile

Kosher salt and freshly ground black pepper

FOR THE LAMB SAUSAGE PATTIES

1 dried ancho chile

1 dried chile de árbol

1 dried guajillo chile

1 lb. ground lamb, preferably pasture raised

2 Tbs. coarsely chopped fresh cilantro

1 Tbs. coarsely chopped fresh oregano

2 medium cloves garlic, minced

1 medium lemon, grated to yield ½ tsp. zest and squeezed to yield 2 tsp. juice

1 tsp. ground cumin

Kosher salt and freshly ground pepper

Lemon wedges, for serving

This spicy recipe is as much an ode to the variety of chiles as it is to the avocado, from the fiery red arból and the green serrano to the mild, deep-red guajillo.

MAKE THE AVOCADO RELISH

In a large bowl, combine the avocados, bell pepper, onion, cilantro, lemon zest and juice, and the chiles. Season to taste with salt and pepper and set aside.

COOK THE LAMB PATTIES

Heat a 10-inch skillet over medium-high heat. Add the ancho chile, chile de árbol, and guajillo chile and toast, turning occasionally, until fragrant and the skins have darkened, about 2 minutes. Set aside until cool enough to handle. Remove the stems, transfer the chiles to a spice grinder, and grind to a powder.

In a large bowl, combine the lamb, cilantro, oregano, garlic, lemon zest and juice, cumin, ground chiles, 1 tsp. salt, and ¼ tsp. pepper. Mix well with your hands and form into twelve ½-inch-thick patties.

Heat a gas or charcoal grill to medium-high heat (400° to 475°F). Clean and oil the grate. Grill the patties, flipping once, until just cooked through, about 4 minutes total. Let the lamb patties rest for a few minutes and serve topped with the avocado relish and lemon wedges on the side.

CHOOSING CHILES

Choose chiles that are shiny and firm pods with strong, uniform color. They should feel dense and heavy for their size; good examples of even the very smallest ones will feel heavier. Avoid chiles that are flaccid, wrinkled, bruised, blemished, or discolored.

Heirloom Bean Tostadas with Crispy Avocado

★ SUSAN FENIGER AND MARY SUE MILLIKEN

SERVES 8

FOR THE BEAN SALAD

Kosher salt

3½ cups (12 oz.) green beans, trimmed and cut into 1-inch pieces

2 cups (10 oz.) fava beans in the shell (3 lb. in the pod)

3 cups mixed canned beans, such as cannellini, pinto, and black-eyed peas

3 Tbs. sherry vinegar, plus more as needed

2 Tbs. extra-virgin olive oil

1½ tsp. agave syrup

1½ tsp. Dijon mustard

2 canned chipotles in adobo, seeded and minced (2 tsp.)

4 medium scallions, trimmed and thinly sliced (½ cup)

Freshly ground black pepper

1 jalapeño, stemmed, seeded, and finely diced (1½ Tbs.)

1 Fresno chile, stemmed, seeded, and finely diced (1 Tbs.)

FOR THE CILANTRO AÏOLI

2 cups (3½ oz.) coarsely chopped fresh cilantro leaves and stems

2 Tbs. fresh lime juice

Kosher salt and freshly ground black pepper

½ cup mayonnaise

Though we call for an assortment of canned beans for convenience, Chefs Feniger and Milliken used heirloom beans, such as scarlet runner beans, to dress up this recipe with color and flavor. If you can get your hands on some dried heirlooms, use a total of 1½ cups dried beans and cook them according to the Basic Beans recipe on p. 171, before substituting them for the mixed canned beans below. For the crispy avocado, make sure to coat the avocado completely with the rice-flour batter. Leaving bare spots will create a greasy taste.

MAKE THE BEAN SALAD

Bring a large pot of salted water to a boil. Prepare an ice water bath in a large bowl.

Blanch the green beans in the boiling water until just tender, 3 to 4 minutes. Using a slotted spoon or skimmer, transfer them to the ice water bath. When completely cooled, use the slotted spoon to transfer them to a platter lined with a kitchen towel, pat dry, and refrigerate until cold.

Return the water to a boil and blanch the fava beans until tender, about 2 minutes. Drain in a colander and transfer to the ice water bath. Drain when the favas are completely cooled.

Peel the fava beans by holding onto the germ end, pinching off the opposite end and squeezing to release the bean from the skin. Transfer the beans to a bowl and refrigerate until cold.

Rinse and drain the mixed canned beans.

In a large bowl, whisk together the vinegar, olive oil, agave, mustard, chipotles, scallions, ½ tsp. salt, and ¼ tsp. pepper. Add the green beans, fava beans, mixed canned beans, jalapeño, and Fresno chile and gently toss to coat. Season to taste with more salt, pepper, and vinegar.

→

FOR THE CRISPY AVOCADO AND TORTILLAS

5¼ oz. (1 cup) rice flour

½ tsp. ground cumin

Kosher salt and freshly ground black pepper

¼ cup red and/or white quinoa

¼ cup poppy seeds

¼ cup black and/or white sesame seeds

2 firm ripe Hass avocados, peeled, seeded, and cut into 8 wedges each

5 to 6 cups vegetable oil

Eight 6-inch corn tortillas, pre-fried or soft

FOR ASSEMBLY

2 cups frisée or curly mustard greens, coarsely chopped

MAKE THE CILANTRO AÏOLI

Put the cilantro, lime juice, ¼ tsp. salt, and ¼ tsp. pepper in a food processor. Pulse until the cilantro is very finely chopped and a paste begins to form. Add the mayonnaise and blend until fully combined. Season to taste with salt and pepper.

COOK THE CRISPY AVOCADO AND TORTILLAS

In a medium bowl, combine 2½ Tbs. of the rice flour and the cumin with ⅓ cup water, ½ tsp. salt, and ½ tsp. pepper to make a thin batter.

In another medium bowl, mix the quinoa, poppy seeds, and sesame seeds. Transfer the remaining rice flour to another medium bowl and season generously with salt.

Working with one avocado wedge at a time, dredge in the rice flour, shaking off the excess. Then dip into the batter to coat lightly, letting the excess drip off. Finally, roll the wedge in the seed mixture, pressing gently to form and completely coat.

Transfer the wedges to a plate and refrigerate until ready to fry.

In a 4-quart saucepan fitted with a deep-fry thermometer, heat 2 inches of vegetable oil to 375°F. If using soft tortillas, fry one at a time until just crisp, about 1 minute, turning once with tongs. Drain on a plate lined with paper towels, lightly season with salt, and set aside.

In the same oil, fry the avocado wedges in small batches until the seeds are golden and crispy, 2 to 3 minutes. Transfer to another plate lined with paper towels to drain. Season the wedges with salt.

ASSEMBLE

Spread a little cilantro aïoli on each fried tortilla and top with a small amount of frisée or mustard greens to create a bed. Distribute the bean salad mixture among the tostadas and top each with 2 avocado wedges and a little more of the cilantro aïoli. Serve immediately.

basic beans

2 bay leaves

2 cloves garlic, smashed

2 to 3 sprigs fresh herbs (such as rosemary, thyme, or flat-leaf parsley)

1 to 1½ cups dried beans, sorted through and rinsed

1 teaspoon kosher salt

MAKE AHEAD

You can cook the beans up to 3 days in advance; let them cool in their cooking liquid and refrigerate them, covered, in their liquid.

Use this basic method to cook any type of dried bean, including cannellini, kidney beans, chickpeas, and more.

Wrap the bay leaves, garlic, and herbs in cheesecloth and tie with twine. Put the beans in a large pot and cover with water by 2 inches (about 2 quarts). Add the herb bundle and the salt. Bring to a boil over high heat. Lower the heat to maintain a very gentle simmer, cover, and cook until the beans are tender (try biting into one) but not splitting and falling apart, 1 to 2 hours depending on the type and freshness the of beans. Cannellini and kidney beans take about 1 hour and 15 minutes; chickpeas may take up to 2 hours (check occasionally to be sure the beans aren't boiling and are covered with liquid; add water if needed). Discard the herb bundle.

If you're using the beans in soup, reserve some of the cooking liquid for the broth.

Rancho Bella Santé

A 120-acre avocado ranch in the hills above Temecula, California, Rancho Bella Santé is owned by Scott and Debbie McIntyre, who also grow lemons, wine grapes, and tangos (seedless mandarin oranges) on their sustainably farmed property. The McIntyres, who raised their family on the ranch, open it for events held by charitable organizations and others, such as groups of avocado and citrus growers (and our *Moveable Feast* episode). A series of farm-to-fork dinners and accompanying ranch tours is now in the planning stages.

The McIntyres' business, Sierra Pacific Farms, oversees the management of more than 5,000 acres of avocado and lemon groves. Launched in 1988, Sierra Pacific operates with a philosophy of fair labor practices, sustainable farming, and environmental stewardship.

Grilled Salmon Wrapped in Collards with Tomato-Mint Salsa and Tzatziki

★ SUSAN FENIGER AND MARY SUE MILLIKEN

SERVES 4

FOR THE SALMON AND COLLARDS

1 packed cup (1 oz.) cilantro leaves, chopped

¼ cup fresh lime juice

¼ cup olive oil

Kosher salt and freshly ground black pepper

Four 6- to 7-oz. salmon fillets

8 large collard green leaves, washed

Vegetable or canola oil for the grill

FOR THE TOMATO-MINT SALSA

1 cup (1 oz.) mint leaves, finely chopped

3 cups red and/or yellow cherry tomatoes, halved or quartered if large

½ cup extra-virgin olive oil

1 large lemon, zested to yield 1½ tsp. and juiced to yield 2½ Tbs.

Kosher salt and freshly ground black pepper to taste →

Though we've adapted this recipe to use salmon fillets for ease and convenience, grilling a whole salmon, as Chefs Milliken and Feniger do, is also an option. In fact, fish cooked on the bone is even more flavorful (see the sidebar on p. 183). For the whole fish, the chefs made cuts along the body and spread the marinade directly in the cavities.

PREPARE THE SALMON AND COLLARDS

Whisk the cilantro, lime juice, olive oil, 1 tsp. salt, and ½ tsp. pepper in a small bowl. Rub the marinade all over the salmon and refrigerate.

Bring a large pot of well-salted water to a boil. Meanwhile, remove the center stem from each collard leaf. Blanch the greens in the boiling water until they become bright green and pliable, about 3 minutes. Transfer to an ice bath to cool completely. Drain and pat dry with kitchen towels.

Remove the salmon from the refrigerator. Arrange 2 collard leaves, overlapping each other, with short sides facing you, until they are the length of a salmon fillet. Place a fillet about 2 inches from the bottom edge. Roll the fillet completely in the leaves. If necessary, trim the edges of the collards so that the fillet is visible from both sides. Using kitchen twine, tie once around the center of the collard packet to keep it closed. Repeat with the other fillets and collards. Refrigerate until ready to grill.

MAKE THE TOMATO-MINT SALSA

Combine all of the ingredients in a medium bowl and refrigerate until ready to use. →

FOR THE TZATZIKI

1 cup plain whole milk Greek yogurt

1 tsp. grated garlic

Kosher salt

1 medium cucumber, peeled, seeded, and grated on the large holes of a box grater (about ¾ cup)

Freshly ground white pepper

1 tsp. extra-virgin olive oil

Small fresh mint leaves, for garnish

MAKE THE TZATZIKI

In a medium bowl, combine the yogurt, garlic, and ½ tsp. salt.

Put the grated cucumber in a medium-mesh strainer over a bowl. Sprinkle ½ tsp. salt on the cucumber and toss. Let stand for 10 minutes. Squeeze out the excess water with your hands and stir the cucumber into the yogurt along with ¼ tsp. pepper, and mix well. Cover and refrigerate until cold, about 1 hour. Season to taste with salt and pepper, and drizzle with the olive oil.

COOK THE SALMON

Prepare a medium (350° to 375°F) gas or charcoal grill. Clean and oil the grill. Oil the bottom of the salmon packets. Transfer to the grill, tie side up, and grill, covered, until the greens begin to wilt and darken and an instant-read thermometer inserted in the thickest part of the salmon registers 145°F, 10 to 12 minutes. Transfer to a cutting board and let rest for a couple of minutes. Remove the twine and serve the salmon, garnished with the mint leaves and accompanied by the tomato-mint salsa and the tzatziki.

[Susan] and I met in a kitchen, of course, thirty-plus years ago. It was immediate bonding."

—Mary Sue Milliken

—— Santa Monica Farmers Market ——

The Santa Monica Farmers Market may be the queen of markets. It's one of the largest, most diverse grower-only certified markets in the United States. And if you pop by one of the four weekly markets, you'll find chefs like Susan Feniger and Mary Sue Milliken selecting fruits and vegetables that will appear just hours later on restaurant tables all over greater Los Angeles.

Launched in 1981, the Wednesday market was so successful that in 1982 the Pico Farmers Market was established to serve the city's west side. The Saturday Downtown Farmers Market opened in 1991 and features the largest number of organic producers. The Sunday Market began in 1995 and hosts food booths, musical performances, and arts and crafts. Participants in the Cal Fresh, WIC, and Senior Farmers' Market Nutrition programs can use their benefits to buy direct from farmers. There are adult and youth education programs and cooking classes. Plus, the farmers' market has partnered with local schools to offer the Farmers Market Salad Bar as a school-lunch program.

Lemon Soufflé with Rhubarb-Vanilla Compote

★ SUSAN FENIGER AND MARY SUE MILLIKEN SERVES 6

FOR THE RHUBARB-VANILLA COMPOTE

1½ cups white wine or Champagne

⅓ cup granulated sugar

1 vanilla bean, split lengthwise and seeds scraped

3 medium stalks rhubarb, cut into ½-inch dice (about 1½ cups)

1 tsp. fresh lemon juice, plus more to taste

FOR THE SOUFFLÉS

1 oz. (2 Tbs.) unsalted butter, softened, plus more for the ramekins

½ cup granulated sugar, plus more for the ramekins

6 large egg yolks

2½ Tbs. all-purpose flour

2 large lemons, grated to yield 2 Tbs. zest and squeezed to yield ⅓ cup juice

1 cup whole milk

8 large egg whites

Confectioners' sugar

This fluffy, light-as-air soufflé tastes like spring, with the brightness of lemon and rhubarb. The compote tastes best when it is served at room temperature.

MAKE THE RHUBARB-VANILLA COMPOTE

In a 2-quart saucepan, bring the wine to a boil and reduce by half, about 7 minutes. Stir in the sugar and the vanilla bean and seeds. Reduce the heat to medium and cook until the syrup thickens slightly, about 2 minutes. Add the rhubarb and continue to cook, stirring frequently, until just tender, about 5 minutes. Remove from the heat and discard the vanilla bean. Cool slightly and then stir in the lemon juice, adding more if desired. Set aside.

BAKE THE SOUFFLÉS

Position a rack in the center of the oven and heat the oven to 375°F. Butter six 6-oz. ramekins and coat well with granulated sugar; tap out any excess. Set aside in a cool place.

In a medium bowl, whisk the egg yolks, flour, lemon zest, and ¼ cup of the sugar.

Bring the milk to a boil in a 1-quart saucepan. Slowly pour the milk into the yolk mixture, whisking constantly to prevent the yolks from scrambling. Return the mixture to the saucepan and whisk on medium-low heat until it thickens to a pudding, 1 to 2 minutes. Strain through a fine-mesh sieve into a large bowl and then stir in the butter and lemon juice.

In a stand mixer fitted with the whisk attachment, beat the egg whites on medium speed until foamy, 1 minute. Gradually add the remaining ¼ cup of sugar and beat until medium-firm peaks form, about 3 minutes.

SOLUTIONS FOR SOUFFLÉS

Soufflés must be baked in straight-sided dishes—in this case, ramekins—to help them rise. Coating the inside of the ramekins with butter and sugar also aids with rising, as the butter prevents the soufflés from sticking and the sugar gives the batter traction so it can climb up the sides of the ramekins.

Stir a third of the whites into the yolk mixture. Using a large silicone spatula, gently fold in the remaining whites until completely combined.

Fill each ramekin to the top, smoothing with the spatula. Run a finger around the inside edge to create a well between the batter and the rim. Put the ramekins on a baking sheet and bake until the soufflés rise at least an inch above the rim of the dish but still jiggle a bit in the center, 15 to 18 minutes. Remove from the oven and dust lightly with confectioners' sugar. Serve immediately, topped with the rhubarb compote.

"My most memo-
rable moments are
of family around
the table. It's the
inspiration for my
restaurants."

—David Lentz

CENTRAL CALIFORNIA

Known as "America's Fruit Basket," Central California is home to juicy stone fruit and plump raisins. Chef Anthony Lamas, a Central California native, knows exactly what to do with them. His farm-to-table philosophy was developed as a kid in the Future Farmers of America, and he's made his Louisville, Kentucky, restaurant Seviche an award winner. Riffing on Latin flavors, Lamas puts local peaches to work in a salsa to top a tender and spicy grilled pork. Los Angeles Chef David Lentz, who's made his reputation as a stellar seafood man at his Hungry Cat restaurants, joins Lamas and the two put in some quality time with fishing poles on local Bass Lake. Chef Lentz is inspired to stuff his fresh-caught rainbow trout with fennel and drizzle the grilled fish with aromatic brown butter. This feast is a delicious snapshot of Central California's finest.

FEAST FAVORITES

Bourbon Mojito
ANTHONY LAMAS, Seviche (Louisville, Kentucky)

Fennel-Stuffed Rainbow Trout with Brown Butter and Dandelion Greens
DAVID LENTZ, The Hungry Cat (Los Angeles)

Arugula and Grilled Stone Fruit Salad with Goat Cheese and Dried Apricots
ANTHONY LAMAS

Spicy Grilled Pork Loin with Peach Salsa
ANTHONY LAMAS

Pecan-Apricot Rice
ANTHONY LAMAS

Grated Carrot and Raisin Salad
PETE EVANS, HOST

Bourbon Mojito

★ ANTHONY LAMAS

YIELDS 1 COCKTAIL

4 large fresh mint leaves, plus more for garnish

2 Tbs. fresh lime juice

1 Tbs. granulated sugar

1½ oz. bourbon

Soda water

Lime wedge, for garnish

By switching up traditional rum for bourbon, Chef Lamas gives the Cuban cocktail a certain spiciness. If your rocks glasses are fragile, muddle the mint and sugar in a mortar or other more-sturdy vessel, then transfer it to the glass.

In a rocks glass, muddle the mint, lime juice, and sugar.

Fill the glass with ice and add the bourbon. Top off with the soda water. Stir to combine, and garnish with mint and the lime wedge.

"It's a good time to live in Kentucky. But this is home for me!" —Anthony Lamas

Fennel-Stuffed Rainbow Trout with Brown Butter and Dandelion Greens

★ DAVID LENTZ   SERVES 4

7 Tbs. extra-virgin olive oil, plus more for brushing

1 medium (about 10 oz.) fennel bulb, trimmed, cored, and thinly sliced lengthwise, preferably on a mandoline

1 medium yellow onion, peeled and thinly sliced, preferably on a mandoline

½ tsp. crushed red pepper flakes

½ tsp. finely chopped fresh rosemary

½ cup chopped fresh flat-leaf parsley

2 tsp. whole-grain mustard

2 tsp. lemon zest

Kosher salt and freshly ground black pepper

Four 10- to 11-oz. whole rainbow trout, scaled, gutted, and boned, heads and tails intact

1 large lemon, cut into 12 thin slices

Cooking spray

6 oz. (about 1 bunch) scallions, trimmed

2 leeks, trimmed, halved lengthwise, and cleaned

4 oz. dandelion greens

4 oz. (½ cup) unsalted butter

½ cup toasted almonds, coarsely chopped

¼ cup fresh lemon juice (from 1 large)

Chef Lentz plays off the mild flavor of trout with aromatic herbs and bitter greens that are bold without overpowering the fish.

Heat a gas or charcoal grill to medium high (400° to 475°F).

Heat 3 Tbs. of the olive oil in a 12-inch skillet over medium-high heat until shimmering. Add the fennel and onion and cook until softened, about 10 minutes. Remove from the heat and mix in the red pepper flakes and rosemary. Let cool to room temperature. Stir in the parsley, mustard, and 1 tsp. of lemon zest. Season to taste with salt and pepper.

Rinse the fish and pat dry with paper towels. Season the cavities with salt and pepper. Stuff each cavity with 3 slices of lemon and ⅓ cup of the fennel-onion mixture.

Spray both sides of an open 11 x 16-inch fish grill basket with cooking spray. Carefully transfer the stuffed trout to the grill basket, placing them side by side facing in the same direction. Close and lock the grill basket. Generously brush both sides of the exterior of the fish with the olive oil and season with salt and pepper. (Alternatively, if you don't have a fish grill basket, you can secure the stuffed bodies of the trout with butcher's twine. Be sure your grill and the fish are well oiled before cooking.)

Lightly oil the grill. Put the fish basket on the grill and cook, undisturbed, until light grill marks appear, about 4 minutes. Carefully flip the fish basket and continue to grill until the fish are just cooked through, about 4 minutes more. Remove the fish from the grill and tent with foil for 10 minutes.

Toss the scallions and leeks with 2 Tbs. of the olive oil, and toss the dandelion greens separately with the remaining 2 Tbs. of olive oil. Season with salt and pepper.   →

GRILLING WHOLE FISH

For cooking whole fish on the grill, the 10-minute-per-inch rule is a good guideline. Whole fish are actually a little easier to judge doneness than fillets, because they are already slit through to the center. Just peek inside the cavity and use the point of a knife to test the meat right next to the backbone. It should separate easily and be just barely opaque. When the fish is done, let it rest for 5 minutes before serving.

Grill the scallions, leeks, and dandelion greens in separate groups on the grill. Cook, turning occasionally, until the scallions and leeks are tender and charred, about 3 minutes, and the dandelion greens begin to wilt, about 2 minutes. Transfer to a plate, tent with foil, and set aside.

In an 8-inch skillet, cook the butter over medium heat, swirling it every few seconds, until melted and the milk solids at the bottom of the pan turn golden brown and smell nutty, about 5 minutes.

Carefully unlock and remove the fish from the grill basket. Transfer the fish to a large serving platter. Spoon half of the brown butter over the fish. Scatter the scallions, leeks, and dandelion greens evenly over the fish, sprinkle with the almonds, and drizzle the remaining brown butter.

Season the fish evenly with the lemon juice, the remaining 1 tsp. zest, salt, and pepper.

Arugula and Grilled Stone Fruit Salad with Goat Cheese and Dried Apricots

★ ANTHONY LAMAS   SERVES 4 TO 6

¼ cup Dijon mustard

¼ cup balsamic vinegar

1 Tbs. honey

3 Tbs. extra-virgin olive oil

Kosher salt and freshly ground pepper

1 lb. stone fruit, such as peaches, plums, nectarines, and apricots, halved, pitted, and each half quartered into wedges

Olive oil, for brushing and for the grill

16 cups (1 lb.) baby arugula

1 cup (4 oz.) fresh goat cheese, crumbled

¼ cup (1½ oz.) pine nuts, toasted

1 cup (6 oz.) dried apricots, thinly sliced lengthwise into strips

4 radishes (about 4 oz.) trimmed and thinly sliced, preferably on a mandoline

If you'd like to add a salty touch to this salad that already combines the sweetness of fruit, the crunch of nuts, the spicy hint of arugula, and the bite of radish, add a few thin slices of country ham, as Chef Lamas did with his nod to Kentucky produce.

Heat a gas or charcoal grill to medium high (400° to 475°F).

In a medium bowl, combine the mustard, vinegar, and honey. In a slow, steady stream, whisk in the extra-virgin olive oil until emulsified. Season to taste with salt and pepper.

Brush the stone fruit with the olive oil and season with salt and pepper. Clean and oil the grill. Transfer the fruit to the grill and cook until grill marks begin to appear on the cut sides, about 2 minutes per side.

Combine half of the grilled fruit with the arugula, half of the goat cheese, the pine nuts, dried apricots, and radishes. Lightly dress the salad and toss to combine. Top the salad with the remaining grilled fruit and goat cheese.

Serve the remaining vinaigrette at the table.

Spicy Grilled Pork Loin with Peach Salsa

★ ANTHONY LAMAS SERVES 6 TO 8

½ cup olive oil, plus more for the grill

½ cup fresh lime juice (from about 3 large)

¼ cup bourbon

8 chipotle chiles in adobo, chopped

2 habanero chiles, seeds and ribs removed, finely chopped (1½ Tbs.)

1 Tbs. minced garlic, about 3 cloves

1 tsp. annatto seeds

3 lb. boneless pork loin

1 lb. ripe peaches, peeled, pitted, and cut into ¼-inch dice

½ small red onion, halved lengthwise and thinly sliced crosswise

2 Tbs. finely chopped fresh cilantro

1 Tbs. apple-cider vinegar

Kosher salt and freshly ground black pepper

Flaky sea salt, such as Maldon

Pecan-Apricot Rice, for serving

Annatto seeds (also known as achiote), which Chef Lamas uses in his spice rub, are an integral part of Latin American cooking for their earthy, slightly peppery flavor and their ability to impart a rich yellowish red color to food. Serve the pork loin with Pecan-Apricot Rice (see p. 188).

In an 8 x 8-inch baking dish, combine the olive oil, 6 Tbs. of the lime juice, the bourbon, chipotles, all but ½ tsp. of the habaneros, the garlic, and annatto seeds. Add the pork and turn to coat. Cover, transfer to the refrigerator, and marinate, turning occasionally, for at least 4 hours and up to overnight.

Let the pork sit at room temperature for 1 hour before grilling. Prepare a charcoal or gas grill fire for indirect cooking over medium-high heat (400° to 475°F). Brush and oil the grill grates.

Remove the pork from the marinade, wipe off any solids, and discard the marinade. Transfer the pork to the hot side of the grill and sear on the top and bottom until grill marks form, about 5 minutes per side. Lower the grill to medium heat (350° to 375°F) and move the pork to the cooler side of the grill. Cook, turning occasionally, until an instant-read thermometer inserted into the center of the roast registers 130°F, 1 to 1½ hours. Transfer to a cutting board, tent with foil, and let sit for at least 15 minutes.

In a medium bowl combine the peaches, onion, cilantro, the remaining 2 Tbs. lime juice, the vinegar, the reserved ½ tsp. habanero chile, ¼ tsp. salt, and a pinch of black pepper. Season to taste with more salt and pepper.

Cut the pork into ⅜-inch-thick slices and transfer to a serving platter. Sprinkle with sea salt. Spoon the peach salsa evenly on top of the pork and serve with Pecan-Apricot Rice.

Pecan-Apricot Rice

★ ANTHONY LAMAS

SERVES 6 TO 8

2 cups uncooked basmati rice, rinsed

7 oz. (about 1 cup) dried apricots, thinly sliced lengthwise

3 oz. (¾ cup) pecans, toasted and coarsely chopped

6 medium scallions, trimmed and thinly sliced (¾ cup)

2 Tbs. olive oil

Kosher salt and freshly ground black pepper

Fragrant, long-grained basmati rice lends substance to this crunchy, fruity blend.

Cook the rice according to the package directions.

Transfer the rice to a medium bowl. Using a fork, fluff in the dried apricots, pecans, green onions, and olive oil. Season to taste with salt and pepper. Serve hot.

Grated Carrot and Raisin Salad

★ PETE EVANS   SERVES 6 TO 8

5 Tbs. extra-virgin olive oil

Juice of 1 lemon

1 Tbs. apple-cider vinegar

1 tsp. finely grated fresh ginger

Kosher salt and freshly ground black pepper

8 large carrots, peeled and grated

½ cup sliced almonds, toasted

⅓ cup pistachios, toasted

¼ cup golden and/or black raisins

1 red Fresno chile, seeded and finely chopped

1 Tbs. ground sumac

½ cup lightly packed fresh mint, coarsely chopped

½ cup lightly packed fresh flat-leaf parsley, coarsely chopped

Chef Evans puts a Moroccan spin on this refreshing salad with pistachios, mint, and a healthy dose of sumac, the tart, deeply red spice that is an essential ingredient in the Mideastern kitchen.

In a medium bowl, whisk together the olive oil, lemon juice, vinegar, and ginger. Season to taste with salt and pepper.

Combine the carrots, almonds, pistachios, raisins, chile, and sumac in a large bowl. Add the dressing and toss to mix. Taste and adjust seasoning. Gently fold in the mint and parsley, and serve at room temperature.

"That's what I love about the flavors of Mexico. Every point along the way it would be delicious, but you just keep going." —Jeffrey Saad

LOS ANGELES, CA

Celebrating Mexican flavors is what this feast with L.A. chefs Brooke Williamson (of gastropub Hudson House) and Jeffrey Saad (host of *United Tastes of America)* is all about. L.A.'s Northgate Market is a provisions heaven for Latin ingredients and sparks ideas for Chef Evans's classic (and very refreshing) ceviche, Chef Saad's "surf and turf" queso fundido and slow-cooked carnitas, and Chef Williamson's crisply acidic octopus salad. For her triple-threat trifle, Williamson brings sustainable espresso to meet Kahlúa® and Mexican chocolate.

FEAST FAVORITES

The Ruby Cigar Cocktail

NICK ROBERTS, Hudson House (Redondo Beach, California) and The Tripel (Playa Del Rey, California)

Lobster and Chorizo Queso Fundido

JEFFREY SAAD, host of *United Tastes of America*

Carnitas with Rice and Salsa

JEFFREY SAAD

Charred Baby Octopus Salad with Pickled Jalapeño, Peaches, Plums, and Cumin-Lime Vinaigrette

BROOKE WILLIAMSON, Hudson House (Redondo Beach, California) and The Tripel (Playa Del Rey, California)

Kahlúa, Espresso, and Chocolate Trifle with Candied Peanuts

BROOKE WILLIAMSON

The Ruby Cigar Cocktail

★ NICK ROBERTS

1 fl. oz. (2 Tbs.) white tequila

½ fl. oz. (1 Tbs.) mezcal

½ fl. oz. (1 Tbs.) cranberry liqueur

Dash of aromatic bitters

1 whole star anise, for garnish

Nick Roberts, Chef Brooke Williamson's husband and co-chef at the couple's L.A. restaurants, uses both tequila and mezcal in this colorful cocktail with a kick. While tequila is made from the blue agave plant, mezcal can be made from any number of agave varieties and often has a smokier flavor.

Combine the tequila, mezcal, cranberry liqueur, and bitters in a cocktail shaker. Fill with ice and stir until chilled. Strain into a rocks glass over a single large square ice cube, filling the glass half to three-quarters full. Garnish with star anise.

Lobster and Chorizo Queso Fundido

★ JEFFREY SAAD   SERVES 8

FOR THE GUAJILLO PASTE (OPTIONAL)

4 dried guajillo chiles

FOR THE CHORIZO

2 chiles de árbol, seeded

1 lb. ground pork

3 slices bacon (about 3 oz.), finely chopped

¼ cup black garlic cloves (about 1 oz. or 13 cloves), finely chopped

1 Tbs. apple-cider vinegar

1 Tbs. guajillo paste, or chipotle in adobo, seeded and minced

1 Tbs. paprika

1 tsp. ground coriander

1 tsp. ground cumin

½ tsp. ground white pepper

Kosher salt

1½ Tbs. duck fat or olive oil

FOR THE QUESO FUNDIDO

4 oz. (½ cup) unsalted butter, cut into 8 pieces

½ medium white onion, finely chopped (½ cup)

1½ Tbs. seeded, minced jalapeño

2 cloves garlic, minced

Ground white pepper

½ tsp. ground cumin

¼ cup all-purpose flour, plus more if necessary →

Making your own chorizo is easier than you might imagine. Chef Saad likes the smoky, dried-cherry-like flavor that guajillo chile adds to the meat mixture, as well as the clean heat of chile árbol. For the queso fundido, he uses a blend of three cheeses: the creamy queso quesadilla, Monterey Jack, and grated Cotija, whose nutty flavor has led to its being dubbed Mexican Parmesan.

MAKE THE GUAJILLO PASTE

In a 2-quart saucepan or a kettle bring 3 to 4 cups of water to a boil.

Toast the chiles in a 10-inch skillet until some brown spots appear and they soften slightly, about 1 minute per side.

Transfer the chiles to a medium bowl, cover with the boiling water, and soak for 10 minutes.

Drain the chiles, reserving the water. Seed the chiles and coarsely chop; transfer to a blender or food processor. Pulse to a smooth paste, adding reserved soaking water by the tablespoon as necessary. Refrigerate in an airtight container for up to several months.

MAKE THE CHORIZO

In a 12-inch skillet over medium heat toast the chiles de árbol until softened slightly, about 1 minute per side. Move to a cutting board, finely chop, and transfer to a large bowl.

Add the pork, bacon, black garlic, vinegar, guajillo paste, paprika, coriander, cumin, white pepper, and ½ tsp. salt to the bowl with the chiles de árbol and mix.

In the 12-inch skillet melt the duck fat over high heat. Reduce the heat to medium, add the pork mixture, and cook, breaking up the meat with a wooden spoon, until it darkens, about 8 minutes. →

¼ cup silver tequila

2 cups whole milk

½ cup coarsely grated queso quesadilla

¼ cup coarsely grated Monterey Jack

¾ cup coarsely grated Cotija

Kosher salt

FOR ASSEMBLY

½ cup ground corn tortilla chips; more whole for serving

12½ oz. fresh or frozen cooked lobster meat

¼ cup fresh lime juice

¼ cup fresh cilantro leaves, for garnish

MAKE THE QUESO FUNDIDO

In a 4- to 5-quart saucepan, melt the butter over medium-high heat. Add the onion, jalapeño, and garlic and cook until they begin to brown slightly, about 3 minutes. Add ½ tsp. white pepper and the cumin and continue cooking until fragrant, about 1 minute. Gradually add the flour while whisking constantly. Slowly whisk in the tequila and cook until most of the alcohol has evaporated, about 3 minutes. Slowly whisk in the milk and bring the mixture to a boil, whisking constantly, until thickened, about 3 minutes.

Reduce the heat to medium low and whisk in the queso quesadilla, Monterey Jack, and ¼ cup of the Cotija. Season to taste with salt and additional white pepper. Whisk until the cheeses melt and become smooth, about 1 minute. Remove from the heat and let cool.

ASSEMBLE

Position a rack in the upper third of the oven and heat the broiler to low, about 475°F.

In a large bowl, combine the ground tortillas and the remaining ½ cup of the Cotija. Mix to combine and set aside.

In each of eight 8-oz. baking dishes, spread ¼ cup of the chorizo mixture, equal amounts of the lobster, 1½ tsp. lime juice, and about ¼ cup of the queso fundido. Top with 1 Tbs. of the tortilla and Cotija mixture, transfer to the broiler, and broil until golden and heated through, about 1 minute. Garnish with cilantro leaves and serve immediately with the tortilla chips.

Carnitas with Rice and Salsa

★ JEFFREY SAAD

SERVES 4

FOR THE PORK

2½ lb. boneless pork butt, cut into 1½-inch cubes

Kosher salt and freshly ground black pepper

3 Tbs. olive oil, plus more if needed

1 large white onion, cut into fine dice (2 cups)

1 medium jalapeño, seeded and minced

1 Tbs. garlic powder

2 tsp. dried Mexican oregano

2 tsp. onion powder

1 tsp. ground cumin

1 tsp. smoked sweet paprika

1 tsp. ground chipotle pepper

5 cups lower-salt chicken broth, plus more if needed

¾ cup fresh orange juice (from about 2 medium)

½ cup fresh lime juice (from about 4 large)

1½ Tbs. agave

FOR THE RICE

2 cups lower-salt chicken broth

2 Tbs. olive oil

1 medium white onion, cut into fine dice

1 small serrano chile, seeded and minced

1 cup of long-grain rice

2 cloves garlic, minced

1 Tbs. fresh lime juice

Kosher salt

For this classic slow-cooked pork dish, Chef Saad uses Mexican oregano, which has a robust flavor that is more floral and citrusy than Mediterranean oregano. Don't substitute Italian or Greek oregano; they have a different flavor profile.

COOK THE CARNITAS

Pat the pork dry and season all over with salt and pepper. In a 6- to 7-quart Dutch oven, heat the oil on medium-high heat until shimmering. Sear the meat, in batches, until it is a deep golden brown, replenishing the oil if necessary. Transfer the meat to a plate lined with paper towels and set aside.

Add the onion and cook over medium heat, scraping up the brown bits on the bottom of the pan, until the onion is translucent, about 3 minutes. Add the jalapeño and continue to cook until it softens, about 2 minutes. Add the spices and stir until fragrant, about 30 seconds. Return the pork to the pan, along with any juice, and add the broth; bring to a boil. Reduce the heat to a simmer and cook, uncovered, stirring occasionally, until most of the liquid has evaporated, 1½ to 2 hours.

Transfer the pork to a cutting board or platter, leaving any liquid in the pan. Using two forks, shred the pork and set aside.

Meanwhile, remove and discard the leftover mixture in the pan, leaving behind any particles that remain on the sides and bottom of the pan. Add the orange and lime juices and the agave and cook over medium-low heat until the mixture is reduced to about ⅓ cup, stirring constantly with a wooden spoon and scraping down any browned bits from the sides and the bottom of the pan, about 8 minutes.

Toss the reduced juices with the shredded pork, mixing by hand to distribute it evenly. Season to taste with salt and pepper.

COOK THE RICE

In a 2-quart saucepan bring the broth to a boil.

Meanwhile, in a 3-quart saucepan, heat the olive oil over medium heat until shimmering. Add the onion and cook until translucent, stirring often, about 2 minutes. Stir in the chile and continue to cook until it

FOR THE SALSA

½ small white onion, cut into ½-inch dice (about ¼ cup)

¼ cup coarsely chopped fresh cilantro

3 fresh serrano or jalapeño chiles, seeded and minced

2 ripe medium tomatoes, cut into ½-inch dice

Kosher salt and freshly ground black pepper

FOR SERVING

Sixteen 6-inch flour tortillas

¼ cup coarsely chopped fresh cilantro

Hot sauce of choice

begins to soften, about 1 minute more. Add the rice and cook, stirring constantly, until slightly translucent, about 2 minutes. Add the garlic and cook until just fragrant, about 30 seconds.

Pour the broth into the rice mixture and bring to a boil. Reduce the heat to a simmer, cover, and cook until the rice has absorbed the broth and is tender, about 20 minutes. Add the lime juice and fluff the rice with a fork. Season to taste with salt.

MAKE THE SALSA

Combine the onion, cilantro, chiles, and tomatoes in a medium bowl. Season to taste with salt and pepper.

SERVE

Heat the tortillas directly on a stovetop burner, on a grill over medium-high heat, or under a broiler until lightly charred. Fold each tortilla in half, transfer to a plate, and cover to keep warm.

Distribute the carnitas, rice, salsa, and tortillas evenly among four large plates. Garnish with the cilantro and serve with hot sauce.

— Groundwork Coffee Company —

Groundwork Coffee Company has been at the forefront of the organic, fair-trade, sustainable coffee movement since 1990, when founder Richard Karno started his Venice, California, rare book and café business by roasting his own coffee. Its current blends, with names like Angel City, the dark, smoky-roast Bitches Brew, and the complex Lucky Jack (named after writer Patrick O'Brian's seafaring character Captain Jack Aubrey), keep coffee lovers coming back to its seven locations around L.A. Groundwork gives back to the community through fundraisers for a variety of organizations.

Northgate Markets

Thirty-four years ago, in Anaheim, California, Miguel González Sr. and his wife, Teresa Reynoso de González, opened their first Northgate González Market, specializing in Hispanic foods. For the Gonzálezes, who had emigrated from Mexico, the business was all about giving their customers foods that reminded them of home and that were harder to find in the United States. They grew, market by market, expanding their offerings, until today the family (many of whom run or work at the stores) has 33 Northgate markets around Southern California.

Among the Northgate specialties loved by both chefs and home cooks are the in-house *tortillerias*, where the tortillas (flour, corn, blue corn, or nopal [cactus]) are handmade with the Gonzálezes' own stone-ground nixtamal masa, and are sold fresh or packaged.

In thanks for their success and to give back to the community that has supported them for decades, the family established the González Reynoso Family Foundation to help fund fellow community organizations.

Charred Baby Octopus Salad with Pickled Jalapeño, Peaches, Plums, and Cumin-Lime Vinaigrette

★ BROOKE WILLIAMSON   SERVES 4 TO 6

1 large yellow onion, peeled and quartered

2 medium celery stalks, coarsely chopped

1 medium carrot, coarsely chopped

1 cup (1 oz.) fresh flat-leaf parsley with stems

6 medium cloves garlic, halved

½ tsp. cayenne

Kosher salt

1 lb. baby octopuses (about 10) cleaned, heads and tentacles separated

½ cup apple-cider vinegar

6 Tbs. granulated sugar

2 red jalapeño or Fresno chiles, thinly sliced into rings and seeded

½ tsp. sweet paprika

Freshly ground black pepper

¼ cup plus 2 Tbs. extra-virgin olive oil

1½ Tbs. fresh lime juice

1 Tbs. honey

1½ tsp. whole-grain mustard

½ tsp. lime zest

½ tsp. ground cumin

1 small clove garlic, finely minced

1 large (about 1 lb.) head romaine, chopped

2 ripe Hass avocados, pitted and cut into ½-inch dice

1 medium peach, pitted and chopped

1 red plum or pluot, pitted and cut into thin wedges

½ cup fresh herbs such as cilantro, chives, and parsley, plus more for garnish

Braising is the key to tenderizing the notoriously tough flesh of the octopus. Chef Williamson uses an aromatic vegetable broth as her braising liquid. Some chefs even add a wine cork to their braising liquid, claiming that it possesses an enzyme that enhances the tenderizing process.

In a 6- to 8-quart stockpot, combine the onion, celery, carrot, parsley, garlic, cayenne, and 1 Tbs. salt with 8 cups of water. Bring to a boil and cook for 5 minutes to allow the flavors to meld. Add the octopuses, reduce to a simmer, and cover with the lid ajar; cook until fork-tender, about 1 hour. Remove from the heat and let the octopuses cool in the braising liquid until they become cool enough to handle, 30 to 35 minutes.

Meanwhile, in a small bowl, combine the vinegar and sugar and stir until the sugar is dissolved. Add ¼ tsp. of salt and the jalapeño. Let the jalapeño soak for at least 1 hour and up to overnight.

Remove the octopuses from the braising liquid, drain, and pat dry. Season with paprika, and salt and pepper to taste.

In a 12-inch skillet, heat 2 Tbs. of the oil on high until shimmering. Add the octopuses and cook until they become caramelized and deep golden brown on all sides, about 5 minutes.

Reserve 6 Tbs. of the jalapeño pickling liquid in a small bowl; strain the jalapeño and set aside. Whisk the lime juice, honey, mustard, lime zest, cumin, and garlic into the reserved liquid. Slowly whisk in the remaining ¼ cup of oil until emulsified. Season to taste with salt and pepper.

In a large bowl, toss together the romaine, avocado, peaches, plums, herbs, and octopuses and lightly dress with the vinaigrette. Transfer to a large platter and garnish with the pickled jalapeños and additional herbs. Pass the remaining dressing at the table.

Kahlúa, Espresso, and Chocolate Trifle with Candied Peanuts

★ BROOKE WILLIAMSON   SERVES 10 TO 12

FOR THE CUSTARD

2⅔ cups granulated sugar

6½ oz. (1½ cups) all-purpose flour

1 tsp. table salt

8 cups whole milk

¼ cup Kahlúa

6 Tbs. fresh ground espresso powder (not instant)

16 large egg yolks

2 Tbs. vanilla extract

FOR THE CAKE

1 oz. (2 Tbs.) unsalted butter, softened

9 oz. (2 cups) all-purpose flour, plus more for the pan

2 cups granulated sugar

2 oz. (¾ cup) unsweetened cocoa powder

2 tsp. baking soda

1 tsp. baking powder

1 tsp. table salt

1 cup vegetable oil

2 large eggs

1 tsp. vanilla

1 cup hot brewed espresso

1 cup whole milk

FOR THE CANDIED PEANUTS (OPTIONAL)

3 cups store-bought honey-glazed or sugared peanuts

½ tsp. ground cinnamon

½ tsp. cayenne

½ tsp. kosher salt

Tempering the eggs is the key to a smooth custard. Adding just ¼ cup of the hot milk mixture to the egg yolks prevents accidentally scrambling the eggs before the custard is cooked. The result is a silky custard that layers up with espresso-fueled chocolate cake.

MAKE THE CUSTARD

Whisk together the sugar, flour, and salt in a 6- to 8-quart saucepan. Whisk in the milk, Kahlúa, and espresso. Bring the mixture to a boil over medium-low heat and cook until thickened, whisking constantly; it will take about 20 minutes.

In a stand mixer fitted with the whisk attachment, beat the egg yolks on medium-high speed until smooth, about 2 minutes. With the mixer running, gradually pour in 2½ cups of the milk mixture, starting with about ¼ cup to prevent the eggs from curdling, and mix until incorporated. Pour the yolk-milk mixture into the saucepan, whisking constantly.

Cook over low heat, whisking constantly, until the mixture begins to thicken, about 10 minutes. Remove from the heat and stir in the vanilla. Pour the custard through a fine-mesh strainer into a large bowl, pushing with a spatula if necessary. Press a piece of plastic wrap directly on the surface of the custard to prevent a skin from forming. Refrigerate overnight.

BAKE THE CAKE

Position a rack in the center of the oven and heat the oven to 325°F. Butter and flour a 9 x 13-inch cake pan or glass dish.

Sift together the flour, sugar, cocoa powder, baking soda, baking powder, and salt into the bowl of a stand mixer fitted with the paddle attachment. With the mixer on low speed, pour in the oil, eggs, vanilla, espresso, and milk. Increase the speed to medium and mix until fully incorporated, scraping down the sides as needed, about 2 minutes.

Pour the batter into the prepared pan and bake until a toothpick inserted in the center comes out with a few moist crumbs, about 45 minutes.

"One word to sum up this dessert? Fun!"

—Brooke Williamson

FOR THE WHIPPED CREAM

2 cups heavy cream

2 Tbs. powdered sugar

2 Tbs. Kahlúa

½ tsp. ground cinnamon

FOR ASSEMBLY

Mexican drinking chocolate, grated

Remove from the oven and let cool completely on a rack. Invert the cake onto a cutting board and cut into 2-inch cubes.

MAKE THE CANDIED PEANUTS

Combine the nuts, cinnamon, cayenne, and salt in a medium bowl. Toss to combine. Add more spices to taste, if desired.

WHIP THE CREAM

In a stand mixer fitted with the whisk attachment, combine the cream, sugar, Kahlúa, and cinnamon. Beat on medium speed until soft peaks form. Transfer the whipped cream to a piping bag fitted with a ½-inch plain tip or a large zip-top bag and snip off a corner.

ASSEMBLE

Spoon enough custard into a 4-quart trifle bowl to make a ½-inch layer. Place some of the cake cubes on top of the custard. Top with more custard. Pipe the whipped cream in several spots around the edges of the bowl. Top with more cake cubes and the remaining custard. Pipe the whipped cream in several spots around the edges of the bowl and add more cake cubes if there is room (there will be leftover cake). Spread the remaining whipped cream smoothly on top. Cover with plastic wrap and refrigerate the trifle for at least 1 hour or up to overnight.

Before serving, top with the candied peanuts, if using, and the shaved Mexican chocolate.

PACIFIC NORTHWEST

Portland and Seattle have their share of rain, true, but all that moisture and a temperate climate make for a long growing season. Pike Place Market in Seattle, as well as many neighborhood markets, along with the Portland Farmers Market, are loaded with vegetables, fruits, meat, and seafood that's done right, done sustainably, and done with great care. It's no wonder cooks and food lovers from all over the country flock to the Pacific Northwest to eat. With six of the region's top chefs, we caught Dungeness crab in Puget Sound and fished for sand dabs; we did market crawls for wild-looking (and incredible tasting) geoduck clams, and snagged strawberries and edible flowers that were bursting with flavor because they'd been picked just that morning. And we met farmers who raise cattle and lamb on that rich pastureland of the Northwest. Did we mention the morels? This is mushroom country, and we took full advantage.

With all these stellar regional ingredients, the chefs cooked up feasts that were both personal and cultural. Greg Denton draws on the flavors of Spain and South America; Gabriel Rucker has a French streak, as does Thierry Rautureau. Tom Douglas can go from Asia to Scandinavia in a heartbeat, and Holly Smith and Maria Hines lean toward the Mediterranean. Yet all of these chefs also take pride in doing things the Northwest way—fresh, earthy, and flavorful.

Strawberries
picked @
6:00 a.m. today

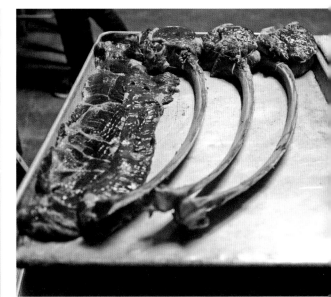

EST. 1990
NICKYUSA
Welcome
Moveable Feast with
Pete Evans

PORTLAND, OR

We could call this episode "When Ox Meets Pigeon," drawing on the names of chefs Greg Denton's and Gabriel Rucker's Portland restaurants. But what we really called this feast that drew on Spanish and South American flavors was "outstanding." Hitting Portland's fantastic farmers market with Denton and Rucker, we gathered fat, juicy strawberries and plump tomatoes, and chose some monster cuts of beef at butcher Nicky. We blended a classic romesco sauce and an Argentine chimichurri, and put together a salad of surprisingly compatible ingredients. But then again, we're cooking with two chefs who are known for their inventive streaks. "If you're a good chef—and you want to stay present—your style is constantly evolving," says Rucker. "I'm not pushing any boundaries. I'm just having fun with what we do." So will you, when you try these recipes.

FEAST FAVORITES

Grilled Leeks with Hazelnut Romesco
GREG DENTON, Ox

Snap Pea and Strawberry Salad with Chèvre and Olive Vinaigrette
GREG DENTON

Flank Steak with Chimichurri, Tomatoes, and Cucumbers
GABRIEL RUCKER, Le Pigeon

Grilled Leeks with Hazelnut Romesco

★ GREG DENTON

SERVES 4 TO 6 AS AN APPETIZER

FOR THE ROMESCO SAUCE

7 Roma tomatoes (about 2 lb.), quartered lengthwise and seeded

¼ cup plus 1 tsp. extra-virgin olive oil

Kosher salt and freshly ground black pepper

1 head garlic

4 dried ancho chiles

1 roasted red pepper, skinned and seeded (5 oz.)

1 Tbs. sherry vinegar, more as needed

¼ cup hazelnuts, blanched and toasted

FOR THE LEEKS

Canola oil for the grill

2 lb. large leeks, about 5, tough outer leaves removed, roots and top 1 inch cut, halved lengthwise, and cleaned thoroughly

¼ cup extra-virgin olive oil

Kosher salt and freshly ground pepper

Chef Denton draws on the Spanish custom of charring leeks, then tucking them into newspaper to steam, followed by a dip into a classic romesco sauce. To avoid any grittiness in the leeks, clean them well by soaking them in multiple water baths and rinsing them in running water.

MAKE THE ROMESCO SAUCE

Position a rack in the center of the oven and heat the oven to 400°F.

Put the tomatoes on a large rimmed baking sheet and toss with 2 Tbs. of the oil, ¾ tsp. salt, and ½ tsp. pepper

Slice and discard the top of the garlic bulb. Put the bulb on a piece of foil large enough to wrap it in. Drizzle with the 1 tsp. oil and season with a large pinch of salt and pepper. Close the foil packet tightly around the garlic and put the bulb on the baking sheet with the tomatoes.

Roast the tomatoes and garlic until the tomatoes are softened and shriveled, and the garlic packet is soft when squeezed, about 40 minutes. Remove from the oven and let cool to room temperature. Squeeze the garlic cloves from the skins onto the baking sheet with the tomatoes and set aside.

Remove the stems and seeds from the ancho chiles. Toast the chiles in a 10-inch skillet over medium heat, turning occasionally, until they begin to darken, about 3 minutes. Add enough water to cover the chiles by 1 inch and bring to a boil. Reduce to a simmer and cook until the chiles darken, about 20 minutes. Drain the chiles and discard the cooking liquid. When cool enough to handle, coarsely chop the chiles.

Transfer the tomatoes, roasted garlic, drippings from the baking sheet, ancho chiles, and roasted red pepper to a blender. Pulse until a paste begins to form. Add the sherry vinegar and the hazelnuts and continue to blend until smooth. If necessary, thin the mixture with up to ¼ cup of water, enough for the blades to move smoothly. With the blender running, add 1 to 2 Tbs. of the remaining oil until incorporated. Season to taste with salt, pepper, and more vinegar if necessary. Set the sauce aside until ready to serve.

GRILL THE LEEKS

Heat a gas or charcoal grill to medium (350° to 375°F). Lightly oil the grill with the canola oil.

Put the leeks cut side up on a rimmed baking sheet. Drizzle them with the olive oil, ½ tsp. salt, and ½ tsp. pepper and gently rub in to distribute the oil.

Grill the leeks cut side down to start, and then turning occasionally, until softened and charred, about 8 minutes.

Remove the leeks from the grill and wrap bundles of 4 to 6 halves in newspaper. Set aside to steam, about 10 minutes.

Remove the leeks from the newspaper and serve with the romesco sauce on the side.

Snap Pea and Strawberry Salad with Chèvre and Olive Vinaigrette

★ GREG DENTON

SERVES 6 TO 8 AS A SIDE

Kosher salt

¾ cup pitted and sliced cured black olives (about 4 oz.)

2 Tbs. seeded and chopped pickled Calabrian chiles in oil

6 Tbs. Champagne vinegar

¾ cup extra-virgin olive oil

2 lb. sugar snap peas, trimmed

1 lb. strawberries, hulled and thinly sliced

1 cup fresh mint leaves, thinly sliced

2 oz. crumbled chèvre (about ½ cup)

¼ cup toasted pine nuts

Edible flowers, preferably nasturtiums (large petals torn), for garnish

Flaky sea salt, such as Maldon

The dressing for this salad gets a kick of heat from Calabrian chile, a spicy, slightly fruity pickled chile pepper from southern Italy. Chef Denton's choice of nasturtium leaves and petals adds gently peppery flavor and a burst of color.

Bring a large pot of salted water to a boil and set up a large ice water bath.

In a medium bowl, combine the olives, chiles, and vinegar. Slowly whisk in the oil until emulsified. Set aside.

Add the snap peas to the boiling water and cook until crisp-tender, about 3 minutes. Immediately transfer to the ice water bath until completely cooled, about 5 minutes. Drain and pat dry with a kitchen towel.

Arrange the snap peas on a large serving platter and top evenly with the strawberries. Drizzle with enough vinaigrette to coat, about 1 cup, making sure to distribute the chiles and olives evenly over the salad. Sprinkle with the mint, chèvre, and pine nuts. Top with the edible flowers and season to taste with sea salt. Pass any leftover dressing at the table.

The salad may be refrigerated for an hour before serving.

"I'm going to show you that salads can be kind of manly. We're hitting it with serious flavor!" —Greg Denton

Flank Steak with Chimichurri, Tomatoes, and Cucumbers

★ GABRIEL RUCKER   SERVES 4 TO 6

FOR THE CHIMICHURRI

1 large shallot, finely chopped (about ¼ cup)

3 Tbs. white-wine vinegar

¾ cup extra-virgin olive oil

¾ cup finely chopped fresh flat-leaf parsley

½ cup finely chopped fresh mint

3 Tbs. finely chopped fresh oregano

3 Tbs. fresh lemon juice

6 medium cloves garlic, finely chopped (2 Tbs.)

2 tsp. ancho chile powder

3½ oz. (¾ cup) crumbled feta

Kosher salt and freshly ground pepper

FOR THE STEAK AND SALAD

2 tsp. ancho chile powder

Kosher salt

2 lb. bison or beef flank steak

3 vine tomatoes or 2 large heirloom tomatoes, cut into 1-inch-thick wedges

½ English cucumber, peeled and thinly sliced

2 Tbs. extra-virgin olive oil

3 Tbs. fresh lemon juice, plus more to taste

Freshly ground black pepper

Canola oil

If you can find bison flank steak, it is much more lean than beef and has a more delicate flavor, but beef flank works perfectly in this recipe, too. Chef Rucker paired the flank steak with an Argentinian chimichurri that begins traditionally, with parsley and oregano, but also includes the novelty of mint and feta cheese for fresh and creamy notes.

MAKE THE CHIMICHURRI

Combine the shallot and vinegar in a medium bowl. Let sit until the shallot becomes slightly translucent, about 30 minutes, then whisk in the oil, parsley, mint, oregano, lemon juice, garlic, and ancho powder. Stir in the feta and season to taste with salt and pepper.

COOK THE STEAK AND MAKE THE SALAD

Combine the ancho powder and 1 Tbs. salt and rub the mixture onto both sides of the steak, covering it completely. Let sit at room temperature for 30 minutes to 1 hour.

Meanwhile, heat a gas or charcoal grill to high (500° to 600°F).

In a medium bowl, combine the tomatoes, cucumber, olive oil, lemon juice, ½ tsp. salt, and ¼ tsp. pepper. Toss well and season with more salt and pepper if necessary.

Clean the grill and oil with the canola oil. Pat both sides of the steak dry with paper towels and brush with canola oil. Grill the steak until medium rare (130° to 135°F), about 3 minutes per side. Transfer the steak to a cutting board, tent with foil, and let sit for 15 minutes.

Slice the steak against the grain and sprinkle with salt. Transfer to a large platter along with the tomato cucumber salad. Top the steak with some of the chimichurri and pass the rest at the table.

CHILE POWDERS

Chef Rucker likes piquillo chile powder as well as ancho powder to rub the steaks. Piquillo peppers have a sweet, smoky flavor.

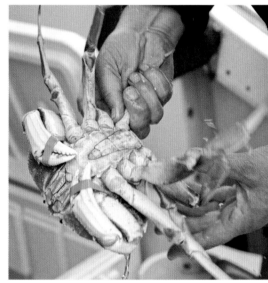

"Dungeness is among my favorites in the world. It's a generous crab, with beautiful flavor and delicate sweetness."

—Thierry Rautureau

SEATTLE, WA (I)

Chefs and friends Tom Douglas (of Dahlia Lounge and 13 other restaurants around Seattle) and Thierry Rautureau (Luc and Loulay), have given radio listeners the lowdown on the Pacific Northwest food scene in their long-running weekly show on KIRO, *In the Kitchen with Tom and Thierry*, which then evolved into *Seattle Kitchen*. Fishing with them on the Puget Sound, with the guidance of Captain Carl Nyman, is a bit like listening to their show—wisecracks sprinkled among cooking know-how and a zest for whatever they dig their hands into. That's plenty during the season for Dungeness crab and sand dabs. A trip to Pike Place Market offered more seafood than we could possibly cook in one meal, but we snagged some fresh squid and took home our catch to create a deliciously briney Seattle feast.

FEAST FAVORITES

Charred Squid Skewers on Garlic Toast with Arugula
TOM DOUGLAS, Dahlia Lounge

Dungeness Crab with Harissa Aïoli and Grilled Veggies
THIERRY RAUTUREAU, Luc and Loulay

Charred Squid Skewers on Garlic Toast with Arugula

★ TOM DOUGLAS SERVES 6

FOR THE SQUID

1 lb. cleaned squid bodies, with or without tentacles

12 or more 10-inch bamboo skewers, soaked in water for 30 minutes and drained

FOR THE CHARMOULA MARINADE

1½ Tbs. finely chopped fresh flat-leaf parsley

1 Tbs. finely chopped fresh cilantro

1 Tbs. fresh lemon juice

1 tsp. minced garlic

1 tsp. smoked paprika

1 tsp. sambal oelek

1 tsp. grated lemon zest

Kosher salt and freshly ground black pepper

¼ cup extra-virgin olive oil

FOR THE LEMON VINAIGRETTE

1 Tbs. fresh lemon juice

2 tsp. minced shallot

2 Tbs. extra-virgin olive oil

Kosher salt and freshly ground black pepper

FOR SERVING

5 oz. (5 cups) arugula leaves, stems trimmed, washed and dried

6 slices grilled garlic bread

Lemon wedges, for garnish

A classic Moroccan marinade, charmoula combines the elements of a cilantro-parsley pesto with the heat of chile-based sambal oelek and the sultriness of smoked paprika.

PREPARE THE SQUID

If the squid bodies have fins (thin flaps) attached to them, slice off and discard them. Cut the bodies in half lengthwise so you have two long tapered rectangles. Using your knife, lightly score the inside of each rectangle in a crosshatch pattern, not cutting all the way through. Repeat this procedure with all the squid bodies. To skewer the squid, thread one rectangle, lengthwise, onto a bamboo skewer, followed by 2 tentacles (if using), then another rectangle. Pick up another skewer and continue until all the squid bodies are used. (You may have some tentacles left over; you can thread them together on a skewer.) Place the skewers in a nonreactive pan.

MAKE THE MARINADE

Combine the parsley, cilantro, lemon juice, garlic, paprika, sambal oelek, zest, ½ tsp. salt, and ¼ tsp. pepper in a bowl and slowly whisk in the oil. Pour the marinade over the squid, cover with plastic wrap, and refrigerate for 30 minutes.

MAKE THE LEMON VINAIGRETTE

Combine the lemon juice and shallot in a small bowl and slowly whisk in the olive oil. Season to taste with salt and pepper. Set aside.

GRILL THE SQUID

Heat a gas or charcoal grill to high (500° to 600°). While the grill heats, remove the skewers from the refrigerator, shake off the excess marinade, and transfer them to a tray. Let sit at room temperature. Grill the skewers over direct heat, with the lid off. Turn the skewers a few times as needed, until the squid is cooked through, opaque, and charred in a few places, about 1 to 3 minutes total, depending on the heat of your fire. Do not overcook, or the squid will be tough. Remove the skewers from the grill.

You can cut the squid and assemble the skewers up to a day ahead, and store, covered with plastic wrap, in the refrigerator. You can also make the charmoula marinade and the lemon vinaigrette up to a day ahead and store, covered, in the refrigerator. Marinate the skewers for 30 minutes before you plan to grill them.

ASSEMBLE AND SERVE

Put the arugula in a bowl and toss it with about 2 Tbs. of the lemon vinaigrette. Arrange the garlic toasts on a platter. Top each toast with some arugula salad. Put 2 squid skewers on top of each toast and drizzle the remaining vinaigrette over the skewers. Garnish with the lemon wedges.

━ **Pike Place Market** ━

Sprawling over 9 acres in Seattle's historic district, Pike Place Market (founded in 1907) is a year-round source for all things edible . . . and then some. Wander the cobblestone streets to check out the farmers' market of local vegetable, fruit, and flower stalls that stand side-by-side with butcher shops, cheesemongers, and four world-class fish markets.

Specialty foods range from spices and fine coffees (the market is home to the nation's first Starbucks®) to homemade pastas to jars of honey sourced from area beekeepers. Bakeries abound, and there are more than 30 restaurants to choose from—serving everything from French crêpes to sushi.

Chefs are some of Pike Place Market's biggest advocates (and customers) and frequently give food and cooking demos, especially in the warmer months. And if you're a record or comics collector, a live-music fan, or in the market for finely crafted objects, Pike Place has a huge crafts and music market (as well as plenty of performances) to dip into before, during, or after all the eating and food shopping is done.

Dungeness Crab with Harissa Aïoli and Grilled Veggies

★ THIERRY RAUTUREAU SERVES 4

FOR THE CRAB AND AÏOLI

2 cloves garlic

2 large egg yolks, at room temperature for 30 minutes

1 cup extra-virgin olive oil

2 Tbs. spicy harissa paste

1½ Tbs. finely chopped preserved lemon

Kosher salt and freshly ground pepper

Four 1¾- to 2-lb. Dungeness crabs

FOR THE VEGETABLES

4 Tbs. olive oil, plus more for the grill

1½ lb. medium asparagus, tough ends removed

Kosher salt and freshly ground black pepper

2 large (about 1½ lb. total) sweet onions, such as Walla Walla or Vidalia, peeled and cut into ½-inch-thick rounds

---

HARISSA

North African harissa is a chile paste scented with cumin, coriander, and garlic, which is used to flavor couscous and kebabs, as well as various salads. It can be quite fiery.

Dungeness crab is revered for its sweet flavor and tender flesh (and is a sustainable choice). In this Moroccan-inspired recipe it's boiled briefly, then paired with a spicy harissa-spiked aïoli and sweet grilled onions and asparagus.

PREPARE THE AÏOLI AND COOK THE CRAB

Put the garlic into a food processor or blender and process until finely chopped. Add the egg yolks and 2 Tbs. water and process until blended. With the machine running, drizzle in the olive oil very slowly until the mixture is emulsified. Once the oil has been added, stop the machine, add the harissa and preserved lemon, and then pulse to blend. Transfer to a bowl and season to taste with salt and pepper. Cover the surface with plastic wrap, and refrigerate until ready to use.

Fill a 10- to 12-quart pot two-thirds full with water. Season with 3 Tbs. salt and bring to a boil.

If the crabs are very feisty, place them in the freezer for 15 to 30 minutes to calm them. Using tongs, grasp each crab from behind and place, backside up, in the pot (if 4 crabs will not fit, cook in 2 batches). Cover the pot and return to a full boil (this may take some time), then reduce the heat and cook until the shells are bright red and the crab is cooked through, about 10 minutes. Transfer with tongs to a large colander and rinse under cold running water until cool enough to handle.

To clean, place a crab belly-side down and grasp the carapace (top shell) from the back and pull off the shell completely. Remove the soft, pointy gills and break off and discard the mouthpiece. Flip the crab over, belly-side up. Using the tip of a small knife, lift the triangular piece of shell (known as the apron) from the pointy end, and break off and discard. Rinse the crab of any viscera under cold water. Place the crab, back-side up, on a cutting board and cut it in half down the middle. →

GRILL THE VEGETABLES

Prepare a medium-hot gas or charcoal grill and lightly oil the grill rack.

Toss the asparagus with 2 Tbs. oil, ½ tsp. salt, and ¼ tsp. pepper. Coat the onion slices with the remaining 2 Tbs. oil, ½ tsp. salt, and ¼ tsp. pepper. Grill the asparagus, covered, turning once, until tender, 6 to 8 minutes. Grill the onion, covered, turning once, until tender, about 10 minutes total. Transfer the vegetables to a platter.

Serve the crab, onion, and asparagus with the aïoli alongside for dipping.

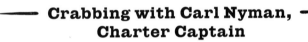

Crabbing with Carl Nyman, Charter Captain

Big, sweet Dungeness crabs populate the Puget Sound and other West Coast waters, and more than a million crabs are taken by sport fishermen each year. Chefs Rautureau, Douglas, and Evans boarded the *Fishwitch* to crab with Carl Nyman, a charter captain based in Seattle's Shilshole Bay Marina. Nyman, who got his first boat in 1980, knows just how to hold a feisty crustacean. Crabbing is on the rise, with the state's recreational harvest more than doubling since 1996, according to the Washington Department of Fish & Wildlife. To encourage better conservation practices, the department has set up a volunteer corps of crab educators that go into the field and give crabbers the lowdown on the dos and don'ts of good crabbing.

"The bold flavor of chive blossoms, nasturtiums, and rosemary blossoms can catch you by surprise. They're tiny and delicate, and then there's that complete flavor explosion." —Maria Hines

SEATTLE, WA (II)

Our second Seattle feast features two chefs who can only be called champions of the farmer. Award-winning Chef Holly Smith, of Cafe Juanita, has put her support of growers and her commitment to sustainability full on into her Northern Italian menu. Chef Maria Hines, of Tilth, Golden Beetle, and Agrodolce, had in Tilth the second certified-organic restaurant in the country. Their meal draws on the finest of Washington land and sea, with Oxbow Farm's edible blossoms, Ninety Farms' sustainably raised cattle and lamb, and fisherman Pete Knutsen's wild-caught salmon that they choose right from the boat.

FEAST FAVORITES

Beef Carpaccio with Carrots and Peas
MARIA HINES, Tilth, Golden Beetle, and Agrodolce

Lamb with Artichokes, Fava Beans, and Yogurt
HOLLY SMITH, Cafe Juanita

Rhubarb Rose Millefoglie
HOLLY SMITH

Beef Carpaccio with Carrots and Peas

★ MARIA HINES   SERVES 4

One 8- to 10-oz. piece filet mignon, trimmed of any excess fat

Kosher salt

12 small young carrots (about 5 inches long), greens trimmed to ½ inch

½ cup fresh peas

Freshly ground black pepper

2 Tbs. créme fraîche

1 Tbs. grated fresh peeled horseradish or bottled white horseradish, drained

1 tsp. fresh lemon juice

1 tsp. finely chopped shallots

1 tsp. finely chopped fresh flat-leaf parsley

1 tsp. finely chopped fresh chives

1½ Tbs. truffle oil

Taking the classic thin-sliced raw beef dish to the heart of the garden, Chef Hines uses fresh, tender peas and young carrots. Not to be confused with the store-bought "baby" carrots, these young ones are slender and naturally sweet.

Freeze the beef until partially frozen, about 45 minutes.

Have ready a large bowl of ice water. Bring a 2-quart saucepan of salted water to a boil. Cook the carrots until crisp-tender, about 3 minutes. Using a slotted spoon, transfer the carrots to the bowl of ice water to stop the cooking, then transfer to kitchen towels and blot dry.

Return the water to a boil and blanch the peas for 30 seconds. Using a slotted spoon, transfer the peas to the bowl of ice water to stop the cooking, then transfer to kitchen towels and blot dry.

Cut the beef into 12 slices. Put a slice of beef between two sheets of plastic wrap and pound with a meat pounder until very thin (almost translucent, but be careful not to tear). Remove the top piece of plastic and season the beef with salt and pepper. Wrap the beef around a carrot and set aside. Repeat with the remaining slices of beef.

In a medium bowl, combine the blanched peas, créme fraîche, horseradish, lemon juice, shallots, parsley, chives, and ¼ tsp. salt, and toss to mix.

Spoon the pea mixture onto a serving platter and spread evenly. Arrange the carpaccio-wrapped carrots on top of the peas. Drizzle with the truffle oil and season lightly with salt.

Lamb with Artichokes, Fava Beans, and Yogurt

★ HOLLY SMITH

SERVES 8

Yogurt sauce is a classic Greek accompaniment to lamb. Chef Smith amps up the flavor, beginning with a garlicky marinade for the lamb and a yogurt sauce spiked with peppers instead of the typical mint. She also adds depth to the veggies with a healthy splash of vermouth.

FOR THE LAMB

2 racks of lamb, about 1¼ lb. each, chine bones removed, and meat trimmed of all but a thin layer of fat

6 Tbs. extra-virgin olive oil

Zest and juice of 1 lemon

10 medium cloves garlic, peeled and lightly pressed to split

2 sprigs fresh rosemary, leaves stripped from the branch

¼ tsp. crushed red pepper flakes (optional)

Kosher salt and freshly ground black pepper

FOR THE VEGETABLE MIXTURE

2 Tbs. extra-virgin olive oil

10 oz. morel or shiitake mushrooms, cleaned (stems removed if using shiitakes) and sliced

6 oz. jar marinated artichokes, drained

1 Tbs. coarsely chopped fresh thyme

Kosher salt

6 Tbs. dry vermouth

½ cup lower-sodium chicken broth

1 cup fresh or frozen fava beans, peeled

1 Tbs. unsalted butter

2 tsp. finely grated lemon zest

Pinch of cayenne pepper →

MARINATE THE LAMB

Place the lamb in a baking dish. Combine the olive oil, lemon zest and juice, garlic, rosemary, and red pepper flakes in a medium bowl and mix well. Rub the marinade into the meat to coat all sides evenly. Cover with plastic wrap and refrigerate for at least 4 and up to 24 hours.

COOK THE LAMB

Let the lamb sit at room temperature for about 1 hour. Position a rack in the center of the oven and heat the oven to 400°F.

Brush off the pieces of rosemary, garlic, and lemon peel from the lamb, and season with salt and pepper. Heat a dry, 12-inch ovenproof skillet over medium-high heat for about 1 minute. Place the lamb racks, fat side down, in the skillet and sear for 2 minutes. Using tongs, flip the lamb and sear for an additional 2 minutes. Transfer the lamb to a plate and pour off the fat from the skillet. Return the racks to the skillet, bone side down, and roast in the oven until golden brown, 15 to 20 minutes, until an instant-read thermometer registers 125°F for rare, or 130°F for medium rare. Transfer the lamb to a cutting board, tent with foil, and let rest.

PREPARE THE VEGETABLES

Heat the olive oil in the cleaned skillet until shimmering hot. Add the mushrooms, marinated artichokes, thyme, and 1 tsp. salt, and cook, stirring occasionally, for 2 minutes. Add the vermouth and cook until reduced by half. Add the chicken broth and fava beans, increase the heat to medium high, and cook, stirring occasionally, until the liquid has reduced by half, 2 to 3 minutes. Reduce the heat to medium low, stir in the butter, lemon zest, and the cayenne, and swirl the pan until the butter is incorporated. Season to taste with salt. →

FOR SERVING

2 cups whole-milk Greek-style yogurt, stirred until smooth

1 jar of hot goat-horn peppers in oil (or any mild or hot peppers packed in oil of your choice)

TO SERVE

Put the Greek yogurt in a medium bowl and stir until smooth and light. Let the yogurt sit for about 10 minutes.

Spoon ¼ cup of the yogurt onto each of eight plates and spread out slightly. Top with 4 to 5 strips of peppers. Pour 1 Tbs. of the oil from the jar of peppers over the yogurt.

Cut the racks of lamb into separate chops. Spoon about ¼ cup of the vegetable mixture over the yogurt. Arrange 2 lamb chops on each plate and serve.

━ **Ninety Farms** ━

Along the banks of the Stillaguamish River, in Arlington, Washington, the grass is sweet, dense, and ripe for grazing, and Linda Neunzig has been raising Angus beef cattle and Katahdin Hair sheep sustainably at her Ninety Farms there for 20 years. Chefs like Holly Smith love the lamb Neunzig produces for its sweet flavor and lean meat, and farmers like Neunzig, one of the first to bring the Katahdin breed to the West Coast, love it not only for the high quality of meat it offers but also because it's a gentle, easy-care breed of sheep—it sheds its winter coat (of hair, not wool), so doesn't require shearing.

A self-proclaimed "farmbudsman," Neunzig is also Agriculture Coordinator at the Snohomish County Economic Development Division, helping farmers and county government meet in projects such as a year-round farmers' market that kicked off in spring 2014.

Ninety Farms sells its products direct from the farm by appointment, holds tours for school groups, and has a CSA, whose members (in Seattle and Lynwood, Washington) are supplied weekly with veggies and meat.

Rhubarb Rose Millefoglie

★ HOLLY SMITH

SERVES 8

2 sheets frozen puff pastry, thawed overnight in the refrigerator

FOR THE VANILLA-POACHED RHUBARB

3 cups sugar

1 vanilla bean, split in half lengthwise with a paring knife

2 lb. rhubarb, cleaned and sliced on the diagonal ¾ inch thick

FOR THE ROSE COGNAC FOOL

4 oz. white chocolate, chopped into small pieces

2 cups heavy cream

1 Tbs. cognac

½ tsp. rose water

FOR THE GARNISH

Candied rose petals (optional)

Millefoglie is the Italian version of the French pastry mille-feuille, meaning "thousand leaves," and is layered with whipped cream and fruit in a style similar to a napoleon. Here, fragrant rose water and cognac combine with rich white chocolate and tart rhubarb to create an indulgent treat.

BAKE THE PUFF PASTRY

Position a rack in the center of the oven and heat the oven to 375°F.

On a lightly floured surface, unfold the pastry sheets. Using a sharp knife or pizza cutter, cut the pastry sheets in half so they are about 4½ inches wide. Place the pastry pieces on parchment-lined baking sheets and pierce all over with a fork. Bake until golden brown, about 15 minutes. Let cool completely.

Using a serrated knife, carefully slice each rectangle in half horizontally to create two layers. With kitchen scissors, cut each layer crosswise into 3 equal pieces, about 3 inches wide. You should have 24 pastry rectangles in total.

POACH THE RHUBARB

Put 6 cups of water in a 3- to 4-quart saucepan, add the sugar and vanilla, and bring to a boil over high heat, stirring until the sugar is dissolved. Add the rhubarb, reduce the heat, and simmer, gently stirring, until the rhubarb is just barely tender but stills holds its shape, 8 to 10 minutes. Pour the rhubarb mixture into a baking dish large enough to hold the mixture in one layer and let cool. Once the mixture is cool, cover with plastic wrap and refrigerate overnight.

MAKE THE ROSE COGNAC FOOL

Heat the white chocolate with 1 cup of cream in a small saucepan over low heat, stirring frequently, until melted, about 10 minutes. Transfer the mixture to a medium bowl and slowly stir in the remaining cup of cream. Stir in the cognac and rosewater. Cover with plastic wrap and refrigerate overnight.

→

TO ASSEMBLE

Using a handheld electric mixer, beat the white chocolate mixture on medium-high speed until it forms medium-stiff peaks.

Gently spread 1 Tbs. of the whipped cream mixture over each of 2 puff pastry pieces. Stack the pieces, cream side up, on a dessert plate. Spoon several pieces of the poached rhubarb over the top cream and drizzle with 1 Tbs. of the rhubarb syrup. Top the rhubarb with another piece of pastry. Repeat with the remaining puff pastry pieces on seven more dessert plates.

TO SERVE

Garnish with candied rose petals, if using, and serve right away.

ROSE WATER

A byproduct of making rose oil for perfumes, rose water has been used for centuries in Europe, the Middle East, and Asia. Because it is very potent, add it judiciously, by the eighth of a teaspoon, so that it doesn't overpower other flavors.

You can find rose water at Mideastern or health-food stores. Since it's also used for cosmetic purposes, look for a label that says 100% pure rose water, with no other additives to be sure you're getting a food-grade product.

"Having a relationship with the person who grows your lettuce or catches your salmon just feels better." —Holly Smith

— Oxbow Farm —

Looking every inch the Northwest farmer in his thick flannel shirt and broad oilcloth hat, Luke Woodward crouches down next to host Pete Evans and picks a purple pompom blossom out of a patch of chive plants. Woodward is the farm operations manager of Oxbow Farm, a 25-acre vegetable and berry farm and fruit orchard in Carnation, Washington, where Pete has come to pick edible flowers for the feast he is preparing with Chefs Hines and Smith.

Woodward also supplies chefs with the edible flowers of familiar vegetables like kale, arugula, and broccoli. These flowers add a sweeter, milder flavor of their respective vegetables, as well as a bright pop of color perfect for dressing up salads. Woodward says he used to consider a crop past its prime when it started producing flowers. "But in farming, you have to be creative. By harvesting the flowers, we can get more produce out of our labors."

METRIC EQUIVALENTS

Liquid/Dry Measures

U.S.	Metric
¼ teaspoon	1.25 milliliters
½ teaspoon	2.5 milliliters
1 teaspoon	5 milliliters
1 tablespoon (3 teaspoons)	15 milliliters
1 fluid ounce (2 tablespoons)	30 milliliters
¼ cup	60 milliliters
⅜ cup	80 milliliters
½ cup	120 milliliters
1 cup	240 milliliters
1 pint (2 cups)	480 milliliters
1 quart (4 cups; 32 ounces)	960 milliliters
1 gallon (4 quarts)	3.84 liters
1 ounce (by weight)	28 grams
1 pound	454 grams
2.2 pounds	1 kilogram

Oven Temperatures

°F	Gas Mark	°C
250	½	120
275	1	140
300	2	150
325	3	165
350	4	180
375	5	190
400	6	200
425	7	220
450	8	230
475	9	240
500	10	260
550	Broil	290

CHEF & ARTISAN LISTINGS

Visit these websites for more information on *Moveable Feast with Fine Cooking* and our featured chefs, artisans, and purveyors.

For more on the episodes, chefs and artisans, recipes, and schedule for *Moveable Feast with Fine Cooking*, visit Finecooking.tv or Finecooking.com/moveablefeast.

Northeast

New York City (Harlem)

Marcus Samuelsson, Red Rooster Harlem: marcussamuelsson.com

Jonathan Waxman, Barbuto: barbutonyc.com

125th Street Farmer's Market: 125thstreetfarmersmarket.com

New York City (Little Italy)

Marco Canora, Hearth: marcocanora.com

Gabrielle Hamilton, Prune: prunerestaurant.com

Di Palo's Fine Foods:dipaloselects.com

Pino Prime Meats: 149 Sullivan Street; 212-475-8134 (no website)

New York City (Midtown Manhattan)

Anita Lo, Annisa: annisarestaurant.com

Andy Ricker, Pok Pok: pokpokpdx.com

Kalustyan's: kalustyans.com

Portland, Maine

Rob Evans, Duckfat: duckfat.com

Sam Hayward, Fore Street Grill: forestreet.biz

Bangs Island Mussels: bangsislandmussels.com

Flanagan's Table, The Barn at Flanagan's Farm: flanaganstable.com

Staten Island, N.Y.

April Bloomfield, The Spotted Pig: aprilbloomfield.com

Seamus Mullen, Tertulia: seamusmullen.com

Brooklyn Grange: brooklyngrangefarm.com

Dickson's Farmstand Meats: dicksonsfarmstand.com

Westport, Mass.

Chris Schlesinger and John "Doc" Willoughby: The duo's cookbooks are available online at amazon.com.

Orr's Farm: farmfresh.org/food/farm.php?farm=1879

Westport Rivers Vineyard & Winery: westportrivers.com

Wilton, Conn.

Tim LaBant, The Schoolhouse at Cannondale: schoolhouseatcannondale.com

Jacques Pépin, chef and cooking-show host: pbs.org/food/chefs/jacques-pepin/

Bill Taibe, leFarm and Whelk: lefarmwestport.com

Millstone Farm: millstonefarm.org

South

Covington, La.

Susan Spicer, Bayona: bayona.com

Poppy Tooker, cook, educator, and radio and television host: poppytooker.com

Bartlett Farm: thegardenveg.com

New Orleans, La.

John Folse, Restaurant R'evolution: revolutionnola.com

Brian Landry, Borgne: borgnerestaurant.com

Covey Rise Farms: coveyrisefarms.com

The Farm at White Oak: jfolse.com

West Pointe à La Hache, La.

Donald Link, Herbsaint: donaldlink.com

Stephen Stryjewski, Cochon: cochonrestaurant.com

Woodland Plantation: woodlandplantation.com

Midwest

Buchanan, Mich.

Gale Gand, SpritzBurger: galegand.com

The Hearty Boys: heartyboys.com

Blue Star Produce: bluestarproduce.com

Chicago, Ill.

Stephanie Izard, Girl & the Goat: girlandthegoat.com

Chris Pandel, The Bristol: thebristolchicago.com

Joong Boo Market: joongboomarket.com

Nichols Farm & Orchard: nicholsfarm.com

California

Central California

Anthony Lamas, Seviche (Louisville, KY):
    sevicherestaurant.com

David Lentz, The Hungry Cat (Los Angeles):
    thehungrycat.com

Healdsburg

Duskie Estes, Zazu Kitchen + Farm: zazukitchen.com

Mark Stark, Willi's Wine Bar: starkrestaurants.com

Davis Family Vineyards: davisfamilyvineyards.com

Redwood Hill Goat Farm: redwoodhill.com

Salmon Creek Ranch: salmoncreekranch.com

Los Angeles

Jeffrey Saad, *United Tastes of America*:
    jeffreysaad.com

Brooke Williamson, The Tripel, Hudson House:
    hudsonhousebar.com

Groundwork Coffee Company: groundworkcoffee.com

San Francisco Bay Area Coast

Ravi Kapur, Liholiho Yacht Club: liholihoyachtclub.com

H&H Fresh Fish: hhfreshfish.com

Outstanding in the Field: outstandinginthefield.com

Temecula

Susan Feniger and Mary Sue Milliken, Border Grill (Los
    Angeles): bordergrill.com

Rancho Bella Santé: spfarminc.com

Santa Monica Farmers Market: smgov.net/portals/
    farmersmarket/

Pacific Northwest

Portland, Ore.

Greg Denton, Ox: oxpdx.com

Gabriel Rucker, Le Pigeon: lepigeon.com

Portland Farmers Market:
    portlandfarmersmarket.org

Viridian Farms (Dayton, Oregon): viridianfarms.com

Seattle, Wash. (I)

Tom Douglas, Dahlia Lounge: tomdouglas.com

Thierry Rautureau, Luc: thechefinthehat.com/
    luc-restaurant-seattle

Carl Nyman, Charter Captain, Fish Finders Private
    Charters: fishingseattle.com

Pike Place Market: pikeplacemarket.org

Seattle, Wash. (II)

Chef Maria Hines, Tilth: tilthrestaurant.com

Chef Holly Smith, Cafe Juanita: cafejuanita.com

Loki Fish Co.: lokifish.com

Ninety Farms: 90farms.com

Oxbow Farm: oxbow.org

RECIPE INDEX BY COURSE